More Fight On!
STORIES

More Fight On!
STORIES

Sam Gipp

DayStar Publishing
PO Box 464 • Miamitown, Ohio 45041

Copyright © 2008
Samuel C. Gipp

No part of this book may be reproduced either in printed form, electronically or by any other means without the express written permission of the author. Said letter of permission must be displayed at the front of any electronically reproduced file.

(Think about it! You spend years writing a book and **thousands** of dollars to have it printed. You then rent warehouse space for them until they're sold. Then somebody puts it on the Internet and it gets copied free of charge. **It's not a question of getting rich!** If the books don't turn a profit, no more books can be written and all the books are rotting in some warehouse.)

ISBN - 978-1-890120-82-5

Check out: daystarpublishing.com

Books by this Author

* Fight On!
* The Answer Book
* An Understandable History of the Bible
* A Practical and Theological Study of The Gospel of John
* A Practical and Theological Study of The Book of Acts
* Living With Pain
* Answers To the Ravings of a Mad Plunger
* Job
* Reading and Understanding the Variations Between the Critical Apparatuses of Nestle's 25th and 26th Editions of the *Novum Testamentum-Graece*
* How To Minister To Youth
* Selected Sermons (Vol. 1 - 10)
* Life After Y2K
* For His Pleasure
* Character Studies in the Old Testament
* How To Get Your Book Published
* The Geneva Bible, The Trojan Horse
* The Reintroduction of Textus Receptus Readings in the 26th edition & Beyond of the Nestle/Aland *Novum Testamentum - Graece*
* Valiant For the Truth (Christian School materials)

Contents

Dedication	i
Preface	ii
Forward	iii
Sitting Down on the Job	1
Left Behind	2
Save Those Men!	3
Heroes, Not Brats	5
Waiting for His Opportunity	6
Everything They Had	7
Taking Care of the One He Loved	8
The First One	9
Courage	10
Sgt. Jasper's Furlough	11
Fragile Bridge to Safety	12
Deep Safety	14
Not Accepting Defeat	16
Stubborn Defender	17
He Kept His Word	18
Struggling Against the Odds	20
He Couldn't Watch Him Die	21
"In God have I put my trust..."	22
"Go For It!"	23
"Let's Get Out There and Save Her!"	24
"Gold is good..."	28
Outnumbered One to Three	29
Christmas in Honduras	30
Better Me Than Him	33
Time to Give Up	34
"But Doris still is living..."	35
Fire, Poison Gas and High Seas	36
One Tough Trooper	38
"Americans are like a matchbox..."	40
"I Didn't Have Time to Feel Sorry for Myself."	41
Desperation At 17,500 Feet	42
Why They Called Him "Great!"	44
The Tale of Two Men	46

Avenging His Brother	47
"I heard pilots..."	50
Light Up the Night	51
Treachery Never Pays	52
A One Night Stand	53
"Now when Ebed-melech the Ethiopian,"	54
Black, Brave & Stubborn	55
An Icy Tomb	56
Aggressive to The End	58
Mad Grab at Life	59
"In God is my salvation..."	60
The Ultimate Emergency Locator Transmitter	61
Brown vs. Brown	65
With a Submarine on His Back	66
Where's the Kitchen Sink?	68
"The American fighting man..."	70
Ferocity vs. Numbers	71
One Man's Fury	72
Stubborn Americans	73
Five Years Stranded on an Island	74
Brain Surgery at 14,000 Feet	76
Loyalty	77
You First	78
Ever the Fighter	79
"Now it came to pass..."	80
The Courage of One Man	81
The Knowledge of One Man	82
"Through God we shall do valiantly:"	83
Commander Gilmore's Capture	84
Courage in a Small Package	87
Do Something!	88
The Deadly Glasses Case	89
The Captain	90
"Yankee Doodle" Is Ours!	92
"Terrorist attacks can shake the foundations..."	94
Savage Attack on Savage Attackers	95
The Warrior	96
The "Berber Banzai"	97
Fifty-four Days on the Mountain	98
You're Only Hopeless When You're Hopeless	100
He Helped Himself	101
Unstoppable Americans	102
Whodathunkit?	103

"We had two or three yards..."	104
Five Months Adrift in the Arctic	105
Hide in the Hide	108
The Impossible Shot	109
"....the Liberties of America..."	110
America's Best Ally	111
Just Doing His Job	113
Repentant Hero	114
"I'm very careful what I do."	116
Twenty Seconds to Hell	117
Pistolareo to the Rescue	119
The Price of Nice	120
"I want to make public acknowledgment..."	122
Gallant Revenge!	123
The Best Defense	125
"Children's children are the crown of old men..."	126
A Father to Be Proud Of	127
Don't Mess With Me	128
Get It!	129
An Officer and A Warrior	130
"O God, thou hast taught me..."	132
Never Too Old	133
Hero Without a Gun	134
Grant's Victory for the South	136
A Tea Kettle, a Pistol and a Good Man	138
A Private Fight	141
"The first half I ran as fast as I could..."	142
The Runner With Heart	143
You Do What You Gotta Do	144
A Brief Stop for Guidance	146
"Who can find a virtuous woman?"	148
A Virtuous Woman	149
Circular Reasoning	151
"Some trust in chariots, and some in horses..."	152
Singin' in the Rain	153
"Before God, I believe the hour has come..."	154
"God give us Men!"	155
"It is the duty of all nations..."	156
More Than a Bridge	157
"We have no King but Jesus"	159
One Man vs. A Battalion	160
Faithful Abraham	162
Lost His Glasses But Not His Head	165

Lethal Grudge	166
The Angel of Marye's Heights	168
The Wrong Man to Wrong	170
"We've Got to Get Those Men"	172
Not Now! Not Ever!	174
The Pigeon Counselor	175
Never Give Up, Never Give In	176
It Was Only Impossible	178
The Woman in His Life	180
"At the time we heard scuttlebutt..."	181
"...I was slated to head for the Pacific..."	182
Fulfilling Her Responsibility	183
Desperate Relay	184
An Appointment With Destiny	186
Aggressive At All Times	188
How The West Was Won	189
A Cry In the Night	190
He Refused to Get Bitter	192
He Walked Home	193
"Better than anything to eat..."	194
Better Than Anything	195
Forced Mountain Landing	196
Foot Race on the Ocean Floor	198
"You know my love, we have to do this."	200
The Desire for Freedom	201
Ole #1124's Last Run	202
Not My Plane, You Don't!	204
The Cannon That Changed History	205
"Shell and Be Damned!"	206
"I thought: You dirty bird..."	208
Because She Didn't Have Her Purse	209
Our Song	210
"Does not such a country..."	211
He'd Had Enough	212
Fake It!	213
An Audacious Escape	214
Say It Ain't So	215
Fight On...and On...and On!	216
The Other Six-Day War	217
"Now these are the nations..."	219
The Lady Was "Unsinkable"	220
Reluctant Hero	222
"The LORD is on my side..."	224

Servant of the Wrong Master	225
The Uncooperative Corpse	227
Save the Fleet!	228
The Slave With A Free Spirit	230
The Crazy Canadian	232
Breaking INTO Auschwitz	234
Brave Leap for Life	235
Pushing Himself Beyond His Fear	236
Six Desperate Men	238
A Son's Love	240
"I love Dad and I didn't want him to get hurt..."	241
Permission Granted!	242
He Chickened Out	243
Only One Hundred and Thirty-Two	244
It Was Their Ship!	245
Sailors Who Never Faltered	246
We All Appreciate Johnnie Frye's Friend	248
No Bluff in Bluffton	249
One Last Brave Act	250
Victory Without A Weapon	251
An Aggressive Defense	252
"I Did Not Tell Them"	254
He Failed	255
"Dear companions, every hope has vanished..."	256
"I've Got Another Idea..."	257
They Tried to Go Over Him	259
Two Heroes at Once	260
He Went Down With His Ship	262
"He was American, he was a soldier..."	264
Army Strong	265
The New York Tea Party	266
A Determined Young Survivor	267
Out You Go	268
Not Settling for Safety	269
Sometimes You've Just Got to Laugh	270
Home Run!	271
Alone in Antarctica	272
"As she was slowly forging by us..."	274
They Saw the Flag	275
Nothing Could Stop Him	277
Nothing Could Stop Them	279
Fall, Fall, Crawl	280
"Without him, we would have lost..."	282

Homeless, Not Helpless	283
The First "Top Gun"	285
One Chance!	286
...And Then Some	287
Takin' er In	288
"....there's nothing courageous in being shipwrecked."	289
A "Human Doing"	290
Determination & a Dull Knife	291
The Old Preacher's Famous Night	292
A Withdrawal of Courage	294
"Come, and let us return..."	295
A Dove Gets "Unsoiled"	296
"Come now,..."	298
"Time and again during the course of that day..."	299
How to Stop a War	300
Index	**301**
Bibliography	**327**

DEDICATED to anyone who has been overwhelmed by the circumstances of life and is looking for something to keep them going. With all my heart I hope this book will be a help to you.

S.C.G.

Preface

As stated earlier in *Fight On!*, there are a few parameters to stories that appear in this book.

I have no desire to trumpet the brave feats of our enemies. I will leave that to the News Media.

I do not wish to dwell on the Civil War. There were brave men on both sides of that conflict. Whenever it is referred to in this volume it will be to testify to generic bravery, (such as the first story in this book), rather than brother-against-brother.

I never cease to be impressed with the bravery of some men, in general, and Americans, in particular.

I hope these stories will be as inspiring to you as they were to me.

Forward

In August of 1973 I broke my neck in a fall. Unfortunately, my doctor never looked at my X-rays so I was dismissed from the hospital just four days after the accident. The fracture wasn't discovered until November. At that time I had C6 and C7, the bottom two vertebra in my neck, fused together.

It wasn't long before I realized something was wrong. Having waited almost three months to have the fusion had apparently caused permanent problems in my neck, constant pain was my life's companion. The neck continued to deteriorate over the years resulting in the collapse of C4 and C5. My hands felt like the bones were crushed and my arms felt like they had been skinned. Headaches and neck pain were the norm.

I cannot tell you how sad it is that the Bible has been shouldered out of American society. In years gone by even non-Christians appreciated and benefitted from its wisdom and inspiration. Today our country needs both of those attributes desperately. I read my Bible daily. Also, over the years I have drifted away from fiction (i.e. the evil villain is going to destroy the world and the lone, brave hero will stop him...with one second left!) The situations of real life are beyond fiction. I confess I have been greatly encouraged by the perseverance of ordinary people who have been thrust into extraordinary circumstances.

I put out a semi-monthly newsletter and took to sharing a brief story with my readers under the byline, "Fight On!" But, I was puzzled when I encountered stories a bit too long to put in my letter. Thus, the first book, *Fight On!*, was born.

Countless people have contacted me to tell me that *Fight On!* was a blessing and encouragement to them. Since I am always reading, a second volume of stories was a natural result. I hope this volume will be a help to you.

By the way, in July of 2008, I had surgery that fused C4 -C7. My arms and hands are pain-free!

The LORD is *a man of* war:
the LORD is *his name.*

Exodus 15:3

Sitting Down on the Job

DURING a Civil War naval engagement, the Union gunboat, *Valley City*, was hit and a fire ignited near the powder magazine. Seaman John Davis, quarter gunner on the vessel, saw an open barrel of gun powder with sparks and embers falling nearer and nearer to it. An explosion was imminent. But no explosion came. The fast thinking Davis ran over and sat on the open top of the barrel. Sparks and burning cinders rained down on the unmoving sailor as he stubbornly remained in place. Smoke rose from numerous spots on his shirt and trousers where embers burned through the material and into Davis' flesh. Exposed flesh blackened and curled, but the resolute seaman refuse to budge. Finally, the fire was extinguished and Davis, severely burned, was taken away and cared for. His quick thinking and selfless determination had saved the ship. He was awarded the Medal of Honor. **Fight on!**

Left Behind

CAPTAIN Miles McTernan was on his 121st mission on January 28, 1973, when the B-52 he was navigator on was rocked by a SAM missile over Vietnam. Two engines were knocked out as well as the hydraulic and electrical systems being badly damaged. The ship was going down. At 10,000 feet over the South China Sea, the aircraft commander set the controls for a gradual descent and ordered the crew to eject. Capt. McTernan, along with the others, did so. The pilot checked the aircraft to see if everyone had ejected. All stations were empty so he himself bailed out. But the airplane wasn't empty. Capt. McTernan's seat, which ejected downward, had misfired and only dropped several feet below the flight deck. His position appeared empty but he was now trapped in the bowels of the dying airplane.

Although alone, and jammed in his damaged ejection seat Capt. McTernan was determined not to go down with the ship. For minutes that seemed like hours, McTernan struggled to free himself as the plane continued its descent to the sea. Finally, forced to abandon his survival pack, he managed to climb back up to the flight deck and dive out through an open hatch into the night air before the B-52 impacted the water.

Capt. McTernan and the rest of the crew were rescued the following day. **Fight on!**

Save Those Men!

ON April 16, 1947, when the *Grandcamp* exploded in the Texas City, Texas harbor, it blew the 438 foot long *High Flyer*, which was loaded with 961 tons of ammonium nitrate, sideways against another Liberty ship, the *Wilson B. Keene*. The *High Flyer* caught fire but there were no firemen to fight the blaze, many having died in the initial explosion. Now the *High Flyer* was in danger of exploding at any moment and had to be pulled from the harbor before that happened.

Employees of the Bay Towing Company volunteered to go in and tow the burning ship out to sea. The tugs *Guyton*, *Albatross*, *Clark* and *Miraflores* were sent in to tow the damaged ship out into the gulf. It was almost 12 hours after the original explosion that the four tugs cruised slowly into a harbor filled with chemical sludge, burning wreckage and dead bodies. By now embers were rising from the broken holds of the *HighFlyer* and raining down on the men on the decks of the tugs. It was clear that the ship could go at any time.

Men from the *Albatross* boarded the burning ship, cut away the anchor chain and attached a tow line to the tugs. Engines roared and the ship slowly began to move. The ship slid silently for about 50 feet and then slammed to a halt and refused to budge. All efforts to dislodge the ship failed. There were still men aboard the *Flyer*. There was no time to waste getting them off. The captain of the Guyton, refusing to leave them, rammed the bow of his tug against the burning ship so the men could jump onto its deck. Then all the tugs opened their throttles wide and made for the channel. It was about 1 AM.

At 1:10 AM, April 17, the *High Flyer* exploded. The column of flame reached over 3,000 feet into the sky. The explosion ignited four 80,000 barrel oil tanks at the Humble Refinery and sent debris raining down on the already torn town of Texas City.

Five hundred and eighty-one people died that day due to the explosion of these two ships. But, because of the selfless courage of the captain of a lowly tug boat none of the men put aboard the *High Flyer* were among them. **Fight on!**

Heroes, Not Brats

TODAY the sons of the wealthy are famous for their extravagance, party life-style and irreverence, but certainly not for their military prowess or patriotism. Not so for a group of elite young men from Yale University during the First World War.

The Yale aeronautical club of the early Twentieth Century was a Who's Who of the sons of the rich and famous. Outlandish, exuberant, dashing, these sons of the richest of American industrialists lived a gaudy life-style full of laughter and flash. But none of them considered himself above the patriotic duty: That a man should be willing to fight and die for his country.

David Ingalls, the Yale hockey star, became the Navy's only ace of WWI and eventually ended up Assistant Secretary of the Navy for Air during the Hoover Administration.

Robert Lovett flew missions with British bombers. Under Franklin D. Roosevelt he was Assistant Secretary of the Army for Air and master-minded the American strategic bombing of Germany during WWII.

Yale's dashing football star, Artemis "Di" Gates, was recommended for the Medal of Honor for landing his flying boat to rescue two downed squadron personnel. As enemy ships fired at his aircraft, he fearlessly taxied to the two men, had them plucked from the waves and then gunned his engines and took off. He was later shot down and captured. He made three failed attempts to escape. He later became Assistant Secretary of the Navy under FDR. **Fight on!**

Waiting for His Opportunity

HIS father didn't love him. He joined the Army Air Corps in 1917. He got his wings March 5, 1918, but was too late to fight in World War I. He crashed his first plane in 1919. He wrecked almost a dozen more times but always managed to walk away from them. He finally left the Army Air Corps having never flown a combat mission, but he was called to active duty when World War II began. Finally, on April 18, 1942, at age 45, after twenty-five years of waiting, he flew his first combat mission for the Army Air Corps ...from an aircraft carrier! That mission was a bombing raid over Tokyo, Japan. His name was Jimmy Doolittle. He later commanded the 12th Air Force in England. **Fight on!**

Everything They Had

WHENEVER man makes an "absolute" statement, God always seems ready to rise to the challenge. The Iroquois Theater was called "Absolutely Fireproof," yet on December 30, 1903, it burned, with the loss of 602 people.

The then new City Hall building of San Francisco was proclaimed "Indestructible," but, after the earthquake of April 18, 1906, only its dome remained standing and that soon came down.

As the above, the *Titanic* was called "Unsinkable." It is said that someone claimed, "Even God couldn't sink it." God was up to the challenge and 1,500 people paid with their lives on April, 15, 1912.

Although the *California*, 10 miles away, was in sight of the *Titanic* and watching her distress flares, the captain thought they were fireworks and never responded. It was up to another ship to play the hero that night.

When the *Carpathia*, 60 miles away, received the *Titanic's* distress call, her captain, a Christian, told his engineers to give him "everything that they had." To increase power to the turbines, he diverted the steam from the heating system. Then, at breakneck speed, he plunged into the night and directly into the same ice field that had claimed the *Titanic*. The *Carpathia's* decks vibrated with the intensity of its overworked engines as its captain scanned the dark waters ahead for icebergs. Finally, four hours later, she arrived and took on all of the *Titanic's* survivors. **Fight on!**

Taking Care of the One He Loved

ON April 3, 1974, a devastating tornado struck Xenia, Ohio, killing 33 people, injuring 1,600 others and destroying 1,300 buildings. Because of the stubborn efforts of Ken Shields, the death toll was not 34.

The twister slammed into the Shield house and totally destroyed it. Slowly Ken dug his way out of the wreckage and then began a methodical search that one-by-one freed his basically uninjured children. When he discovered his wife, Pam, the news was not as good.

Ken found his wife lying helplessly in a pool of her own blood with a piece of wood driven into her neck. Tenderly he picked her up and carried her to the family car to take her to the hospital. But when he got to the car he found that, due to the low air pressure within the tornado, all four tires had exploded. Since this was the woman he loved, he would not be stopped. He gently laid Pam in the car and started out over the debris-laden streets on four flat tires. As the car bucked and bumped along, the tires tore off the rims one-by-one. Desperately trying to keep the car moving, while restraining Pam from removing the wood from her neck, Ken bumped on until a police car stopped him to see why he was driving without tires. Pam was quickly loaded into the cruiser and rushed to the hospital. Her life was saved by the man who loved her too much to be stopped by four flats tires. **Fight on!**

The First One

THERE were only 12 Army Special Forces soldiers in the Vietnamese village of Nam Dong on the night of July 5, 1964, when it was attacked by an overwhelming number of Viet Cong guerillas. The A-Team leader was 30 year old Captain Roger Donlon. His team sergeant was 45 year old Gabriel "Pop" Alamo, a veteran of World War II. The camp was training about 300 irregular Vietnamese troops. At about 2:30 AM a Viet Cong force of about 900 men, aided by over 100 spies among the camp's 300 trainees, struck the Special Forces camp. As Capt. Donlon headed for a mortar pit, he was wounded by an enemy mortar round that blew off one of his shoes. As he prepared to help the crew, another round hit, wounding him in the left arm, ripping his stomach open and blowing away his other shoe. Nevertheless, Donlon crawled to another mortar pit in which all the men had been wounded. He provided covering fire as they pulled back. He had to leave the body of Sgt. Alamo. Capt. Donlon then tore up his shirt to bandage two wounded men and stuffed the rest in his abdomen to help hold in his intestines. He then reestablished the mortar, crawled back to the abandoned pit for ammunition while being wounded again in the leg by a grenade. In spite of his wounds, Donlon directed the camp's defense for five hours, being further wounded in the face, leg and his entire body. Finally, dawn, and reinforcements came; the camp had held. Capt. Donlon lived to finish his tour and to ultimately retire from the Army as a colonel. But first he received the first Medal of Honor awarded in Vietnam. **Fight on!**

COURAGE

I love the man who dares to face defeat
And risks a conflict with heroic heart;
I love the man who bravely does his part
Where right and wrong in bloody battle meet.

When bugles blown by cowards sound retreat,
I love the man who grasps his sword again
And sets himself to lead his fellow-men
Far forward through battle's din and heat.

For he who joins the issue of life's field
Must fully know the hazard of the fray,
And dare to venture ere he hope to win;
Must choose the risk and then refuse to yield
Until the sunset's light shall close the day
And God's great city lets the victor in.

Ozora S. Davis

Sgt. Jasper's Furlough

HOW gallant can one man be? Sgt. William Jasper was definitely a unique individual. He retrieved the fallen flag at Fort Moultrie, helped free a dozen colonial prisoners and then repeated his courageous action with the flag at the battle for Savannah, Georgia, where, due to the poor leadership of a French commanding officer, 1,200 French and American soldiers were killed before retreat was sounded.

Three times the American flagstaff was shot down by British fire. Three times Sgt. Jasper rushed to the fallen colors and raised them defiantly. But when retreat was sounded, the flag was abandoned. It was now closer to the advancing British than to the American lines. Sgt. Jasper could not bear the thought of his flag falling to the enemy. "They shall never fall into British hands, not while I am alive!" he proclaimed and then charged to their rescue. Bullets kicked up dirt clouds at his feet as he darted across the battlefield. Untouched, he reached the flag and, as his hands tore it from the staff, he was shot through the lungs. Bleeding terribly he clutched the flag to his chest, staggered back to his retreating lines and passed it to his commanding officer, stating, "I believe I have got my furlough." Confused, the officer asked to where he was being furloughed.

"To go home.....to Heaven."

The dying man asked his commander to give his sword to his father. "Tell him I have never dishonored it..."

That evening Sgt. Jasper got his furlough. **Fight on!**

Fragile Bridge to Safety

SAO PAULO is Brazil's largest city. In 1974, the 25 story Joelma Building was one of its newest buildings. On February 1, 1974, it became the site of one of Brazil's greatest tragedies.

Six hundred and fifty people were in the building that day when a fire broke out on the eleventh floor. Those below the fire quickly escaped. But 350 people were cut off above the blaze as it traveled up the structure. Many tried dashing down the stairwells through the flames only to be overcome and die. Others huddled on the roof, begging circling helicopters to rescue them though the heat was so intense that they could not land. While spectators looked on in horror, many victims, trapped by the flames, chose to leap to their deaths rather than burn. All told, 227 people were to die in the conflagration.

Worst of all was the discovery that the fire department was ill-prepared to fight a blaze in a modern skyscraper. Their ladders weren't long enough nor their hoses powerful enough to reach the upper floors. They were reduced to holding up signs that assured the victims, "Courage, we are with you."

But not all firemen were thwarted. Some entered adjoining buildings and shot lines over to the burning structure. Then they crossed the thin strand and with hanging on to their backs, hauled individuals to safety,.

Fireman Jose' Rufino was just making a return trip with a man desperately gripping his back when, many floors above him, a hopeless victim cast himself out into eternity to avoid being incinerated. The falling man plummeted right into Rufino and his package and then bounced off and continued his fall. The grip of the man on Rufino's back was broken and he too fell to his death. Rufino clung desperately to the tiny rope trying to keep from becoming the third victim of the incident. Finally, he steadied himself and made his way to safety. After he was checked over, he was back on the rope, bringing helpless passengers to safety. Eighteen times Jose' Rufino made that trip successfully. **Fight on!**

Deep Safety

KELLOGG, Idaho, was the site of a tragic fire in one of its silver mines in 1972. The mine descended almost a mile underground and was a sprawling entity that had been likened to a huge underground apartment house.

On May 2, 700 feet below the surface, a fire started by spontaneous combustion filled the mine shafts with deadly smoke. While the fire raged, rescue teams descended into the depths of the mine looking for survivors but returning only with bodies. All told, 91 men died in the accident; 93 were missing.

When the smoke first filled the shafts, Tom Wilkenson and Tom Flory and seven other miners tried to get out but were trapped below due to inoperable elevators. They knew they had only one hope - to go deeper into the mine. They had been told that, in the event of a fire, fresh air would be pumped into the lowest portions. It was.

The nine men struggled through the heat, smoke and deadly carbon monoxide, racing downward, hoping to reach good air before they were asphyxiated.

One Tom fell and the other dragged him to the safety of a lower shaft 4,800 feet below the surface. Having secured his co-worker, he then stumbled back for the others. But, one-by-one, he found only seven bodies. He then returned to his partner and waited. A day passed. Then two. Three. Then four. The lights on their helmets finally faded and died. The men groped in the darkness and found other miners' lunch pails and fed themselves in the inky blackness. Five days, then six. After a week, the two tired, desperate men heard the voices of a search party looking for the last two bodies of the 93 miners who had been trapped by the fire. To their shock and joy they found them alive! The men were sent to the surface in a rescue capsule to the delight of their families and fellow workers. They were the only two survivors. Refusing to give up, they had struggled on through smoke, heat and darkness as their lungs cried for air until they had finally made it to a safe haven deep beneath the surface of the earth. **Fight on!**

Not Accepting Defeat

ROBLEY D. Evans lied. He was only 13 years old but said he was older and thus secured an appointment to the Naval Academy. Due to the Civil War, he graduated early and was commissioned an acting ensign in 1863.

On January 15, 1865, while leading a U.S. Marine assault on Fort Fisher, Evans was shot and wounded four times in one foot and in both legs. These were the days when the standard rule for men wounded by the huge 58 caliber bullets of that era was, "If it's in an arm or leg, cut it off. If it's in the body, let him alone, he's gonna die."

Miraculously, young Evans did not lose his legs. But due to these wounds, he was medically discharged from the Navy. Since serving in the Navy was all Evans loved, all he lived for, he appealed his discharge to Congress and, amazingly, was reinstated.

The Civil War was over but the tenacious young Evans' naval career was not. July of 1898 found him in the harbor of Santiago, Cuba, commanding the battleship, *Iowa*, as it fired the first shots at the Spanish fleet in the battle for that harbor.

Robley Evans still wasn't finished. In 1906 he commanded the historic 'round - the- world cruise of the "Great White Fleet."

He saw all this action because years earlier he had refused to accept the turn of events from wounds received in battle. **Fight on!**

Stubborn Defender

AL Schmid was with a three man machine gun crew guarding against a Japanese counterattack as the Marines tried to consolidate their foothold on Guadalcanal in 1942. His position faced the most likely approach across the Tenaru River. He had contracted blood poisoning and had been ordered out of the area to a hospital for treatment. But when the Japanese attack was imminent he begged to return to his outfit for one more night. That night over 800 Japanese soldiers swarmed across the river. One of his fellow machine gunners was killed. The other was wounded. For hours through the night, Schmid loaded and fired the gun alone. Shrapnel punctured the water jacket on his gun but Schmid kept fighting with the barrel glowing. Suddenly, a grenade exploded and dropped him. Taken for dead he was laid with other bodies to be buried. He managed to feebly wiggle his hand and was taken to a hospital ship. He lost an eye but recovered from his wounds. **Fight on!**

He Kept His Word

IT was a rainy April morning in 1951 when Melvin J. Shadduck's observation plane entered a narrow North Korean valley, never to leave it. The little plane was rocked by small arms fire and, try to save it as he might, Shadduck was forced to crash land, injuring an arm. He was immediately surrounded by Chinese Communist soldiers and taken prisoner. But Shadduck had no intention of remaining a guest of the Chinese Communists. He quickly attempted an escape and was just as quickly recaptured. He was then placed with five other POW's and marched north. They were headed for China. One of the wounded soldiers died on the way. Shadduck knew they might never be released if they crossed into China. (Korean War prisoners who were taken to China were never released when the war ended.) Shadduck was the ranking officer and planned another escape. He promised the other sickly prisoners that if he succeeded he would organize a mission to rescue them. One night he silently slipped out of the camp and moved south, eventually arriving at the Imjin River. Wide and turbulent, it presented quite an obstacle. He followed the northern bank looking for a way to cross and almost walked into a North Korean outpost. He cautiously skirted this and continued on. He found a small boat and attempted a crossing but the wild river drove him back to the northern shore. Suddenly he happened upon a small Korean boy whose family graciously fed him and helped him plan his move south. On the set day, Shadduck and the lad started out and, evading North

Korean patrols, finally ran into United Nations' troops on patrol.

Back at the UN camp, Shadduck informed them of the remaining prisoners and urged an immediate rescue mission. An Army colonel jumped at the idea and soon thereafter an armored assault force moved out with Shadduck as their guide. They crossed enemy lines and assaulted the prison camp, scattering its defenders. Then they called in helicopters to remove those too weak to travel, turned around and headed home with the rest. Melvin Shadduck had kept his word. **Fight on!**

Struggling Against the Odds

ON May 8, 1902, Mt. Pelee, on the Caribbean island of Martinique, exploded. The coastal town of St. Pierre lay in its path. Rather than lava, Mt. Pelee engulfed the town of 30,000 people with a searing cloud of ash with a temperature of over 2000 degrees. Those who were not burned to death died from breathing the super-heated air. The town was wiped off the map.

Leon Compere-Leandre, a 28 year old shoemaker, was sitting on his porch when the blast hit. Feeling his flesh sizzling, he fought his way up the steps, into the house and fell onto a table. Others, horribly burned, staggered in, fell on the floor around him and died. Leandre felt the urge to fall to the floor and let death take him, but instead he staggered into his room and threw himself onto his bed, buried his face in his pillow and waited for death as the ground shook the house violently. Apparently that action prevented his lungs from being fatally seared and he survived. He was one of the only two survivors out of the town's 30,000 inhabitants. **Fight on!**

He Couldn't Watch Him Die

FRED West was with a crew that was blasting right-of-ways through Sequoia National Park in August, 1930. A few days into that month, a rock thrown by a dynamite blast struck him in the hip. It appeared that no damage had been done to him.

On August 7, West lit a fuse that would ignite twelve huge explosive charges. Then, as he was about to run to safety, he was suddenly struck with paralysis and fell helpless, directly in the path of the explosions. The next few seconds would be his last. But from a distance, one of West's co-workers, Marvin Murphy, couldn't stand by and watch him die. With the fuse burned beyond reach, Murphy left the safety of his position and sprinted to the helpless man. As the fire reached the charges, Murphy dragged West to the safety of some nearby abutments as 12 blasts resounded. Rocks and rubble pelted the area but West and his rescuer were safe. West recovered from the illness. **Fight on!**

*In God have I put my trust:
I will not be afraid what man
can do unto me.*

Psalm 56:11

Go For It!

ON September 11, 2001, as Flight 93 winged its way toward a diabolical appointment with the Capitol Building in Washington, D.C., various passengers manned their cell phones and called those they loved.

Jeremy Glick called his wife, Lyz. They discussed Jeremy's plight and its probable outcome. As they were speaking, Todd Beamer and other passengers began to formulate a plan to rush the highjackers. They decided to take a vote.

"What do you think we should do?" Jeremy quizzed his wife, realizing the most likely outcome was for the airplane to crash. The mother of their three month old baby daughter never hesitated. "Go for it!"

They did. They foiled the highjackers at the cost of their own lives, and the brave widow knows her man had a part in defending their country. **Fight on!**

"Let's Get Out There and Save Her!"

THE keel for the *USS Benjamin Franklin* was laid December 7, 1942, one year after the Japanese sneak attack on Pearl Harbor. She was launched October 14, 1943, and sent to the Pacific to avenge that attack. She carried a crew of 2,500 men.

On October 29, 1944, while in the Leyte Gulf after the big Japanese attack on the landing fleet there, the *Franklin* was subject to the first Kamikaze attack of the war. A Japanese Zeke dove out of the clouds and right into the flight deck. The explosion killed 54 sailors and tore a thirty foot hole in the deck. Fires raged below, and on, the flight deck. Twenty minutes after the attack gasoline fumes exploded below deck causing more even damage. Water from the fire fighting efforts was two feet deep on the lower decks causing the Franklin to list dangerously to starboard.

Finally the fires were extinguished, but damage was too extensive to be repaired in the South Pacific, so "Big Ben" had to sail to Bremerton, Washington, for repairs. She arrived in late November, 1944, was overhauled and sailed again on January 31, 1945. She arrived at Pearl Harbor on February 12 ans returned to action March 3, 1945.

Franklin was made the flagship of Task Force 58-2 which was conducting air operation off the very shores of Japan. At 7:05AM March 19, 1945, as she was in the process of launching her planes just sixty miles off the Japanese coast, a twin engine Japanese bomber suddenly dove from the clouds and dropped two 500 lb. bombs directly onto the flight deck. The first blew the forward aircraft elevator high into the sky and dropped it askew back into its opening in the flight deck. Burning aviation gas below and on deck set aircraft to exploding. Next, the ready ammunition lockers blew up. Soon 40,000 gallons of gas were burning all over the ship. The burning fuel formed a fiery "water fall" cascading from within the ship into the sea. Men were incinerated. In the midst of this floating "Hell", Fire Marshall Stan Graham, called his desperate men together, "Boys, we got pressure on the lines, we got hoses, let's get out there and save her!"

At 7:25, just 20 minutes after the attack, damage was so bad and fires so out of control that Admiral Ralph Davison advised the ship's captain, Leslie Gehres, to abandon ship. As shells exploded and smoke rose a mile into the sky, Captain Gehres chose to try to save his grievously wounded ship. He knew if he abandoned ship the *Franklin* would then be sunk by torpedoes from U. S. ships. He feared there were men trapped below who would go down with it. (He was proven right. Five men were cut off in the aft of the ship and weren't rescued until 17 hours after the attack. They would have gone down with it had it been abandoned.)

Below deck, hundreds of men were trapped by the flames. They dogged-down hatches and prayed for rescue as the ship was rocked by the explosion of live bombs cooking off. Once again in her short life, the *Franklin* found herself listing hazardously to starboard. Number One Fireroom went offline. Fires raged the entire length of the ship. The ship's speed dropped to 8 knots as the engine room had to be abandoned. Finally she lay dead in the water. It seemed the end was near for *Big Ben.*

But due to the valiant efforts of the crew, the hanger deck fires were almost under control by noon and men fought their way back toward the engineering spaces to try to relight the boilers and get the ship underway. While these efforts were going on another Japanese bomber suddenly dropped from the clouds and turned towards the *Franklin*. Every ship in the area fired at the invader. Aboard the *Franklin*, the only functioning quad 40mm gun hammered away pitifully at the incoming bomber. Just before the plane was shot from the sky it released a lone 500 lb. bomb toward the embattled ship. Every eye watched as the bomb descended. Every man held his breath - praying. They watched as the bomb plunged into the water just 200 yards from the *Franklin*.

By 2 PM the *Franklin* was under tow, but her speed was only 3½ knots. At that rate the big ship would take over a week to escape Japanese waters. Long before that happened Japanese planes would hurt her down and sink her.

While firemen gained the upper hand on the flames above deck, engineers were having some success of their own below. Lights flickered back on and by midnight steam was up in Fireroom Number 3. By 10 AM on the 20th, *Big Ben* was making 15 knots on her own.

All day long Japanese planes searched for the ship in hopes of finishing her off. Then at 2:30 PM they found her. Enemy planes dove toward the *Franklin* as the guns of the accompanying warships swatted them down. Then one lone plane got through. As he lined up on his bomb run, the ship's lone quad 40 and a few 20mm guns literally exploded into action. So startled was the enemy pilot that he hauled back on the stick just as he released his bomb and it missed the ship by less than 100 feet.

All day long the Japanese swarmed above the stricken ship while U.S. Navy Hellcats fought them off. Meanwhile, engineers coaxed enough power out of her two (of four) firerooms to push her up to 20 knots.

On March 25, 1945, the *USS Franklin*, her hull blackened by flames, dropped anchor in Ultihi harbor for a very temporary respite. The next morning she departed for Pearl Harbor, arriving there on April 3, just one short but brutal month after she had left. Her journey was not over. After five days of temporary repair, she departed Pearl, transited the Panama Canal and headed up the East Coast for the repair facility at the Brooklyn Navy Yard. Twenty-seven days later, on April 30 she, with all hands at salute, passed the Statue of Liberty. Her decks were a shambles. Her hull was rusty-red where the paint had been burned off. She had lost 724 sailors from her near fatal attack. But *"Big Ben"* was home at last.

She was repaired. But it was too late for the gallant ship to re-enter the war, so, *Big Ben* was retired. In her short career she had sunk 160 ships, downed 338 enemy aircraft and launched 3,971 air sorties. The *U S S Franklin* was in service less than two years but in that short period of time she became the most decorated ship in U.S. Naval history. **Fight on!**

"Gold is good in its place; but, loving, brave, patriotic men are better than gold."

Abraham Lincoln

Outnumbered One to Three

IN 1891 Mexico was experiencing the Garza rebellion, an attempt to overthrow the government of Mexican President Diaz. Mexican revolutionaries, while running from their own authorities, often crossed into Texas to evade capture.

On December 31, 1891, Private Allen Walker of the 3rd U.S. Cavalry was delivering dispatches between two posts when he happened upon three armed Mexicans, also on horseback. Knowing they were defying the laws of both countries, and not caring that he was outnumbered, Pvt. Walker said to himself, "These fellows may trifle with the laws of their own country, but by God they won't do it with mine!" The enraged trooper dashed up to the three and demanded their surrender. In an instant the shooting commenced and soon one Mexican was captured and another wounded, while the third had fled. The three had been outnumbered by the one.

But that's not the end of the story. Pvt. Walker's prisoners had papers on them that detailed plans for an invasion of the United States, an invasion which his courageous action had prevented. **Fight on!**

Christmas in Honduras

REVOLUTIONS were plentiful in Honduras in the late nineteenth and early twentieth centuries. On April 14, 1897, revolutionaries had commandeered a train on a 40 mile long railroad that served the banana plantations. They gave the engineer a choice: He was free to remain on the train and operate it for them or he was free to be shot. He chose the former.

Soon the train was halted at a trestle by a force of federal troops. As the two forces battled from opposite ends of the trestle, the federales launched an assault across it. Just as the rebels were about to be overrun, the newly appointed rebel train engineer dashed from the engine, picked up a rifle and blazed away at the Honduran army troops with such hot and accurate fire that the attack was broken and the *federales* fled. Thus, the Battle of Laguna Trestle ended, but the bizarre military career of Leon "Lee" Christmas began.

Lee Christmas, born in New Orleans, had been an engineer in the United States. His career ended when he failed a newly instituted color blindness test. He heard railroading jobs were available in Central America and landed in Honduras in November of 1894. If it were not for the episode at Laguna trestle three years later, he may have finished his life as an anonymous railroad engineer, carrying bananas across Honduras. But due to his performance in that battle, in 1902 Honduran President, Terrencio Sierra, appointed Christmas, who had become somewhat of a legend for the Laguna trestle affair and for having survived a shotgun blast to the chest two years later, as a colonel and chief of police in the capital city of Tegucigalpa. Unfortunately, Sierra treacherously backed out on an agreement to turn the presidency over to Manuel Bonilla. So Christmas and his entire 185 man police force joined Bonilla and the Revolution of 1903 was on!

During an attack on the capital city, Col. Christmas flanked and ambushed a force of *federale* troops and killed or captured over 100 men. Sierra fled, Bonillo became president and the engineer, turned military commander, became a brigadier general.

In 1906, the Nicaraguan army invaded Honduras and Christmas had a leg shattered by a bullet in an ensuing battle. Bonilla's government collapsed and the new president, Miguel Davila had no use for Christmas.....but Bonillo did. The 1910 edition of the seemingly endless Honduran revolution began with Christmas commanding Bonilla's army of fifteen men armed with 100 rifles. But as the force sailed on Bonilla's navy, a 30 foot sloop, they met up with a Honduran navy ironclad. Thus ended the fleeting Revolution of 1910.

Not to worry; another year, another revolution. Bonilla and Christmas managed to make it back to New Orleans where Christmas soon sailed off in Bonilla's new navy, an 80 foot steam-powered yacht which soon rendezvoused with Bonilla's new army of thirty men. Things were looking up. The Revolution of 1911 was definitely on.

After capturing a small island, the little army sailed into Trujillo harbor where General Christmas' brilliant placement of his machines guns routed the Honduran defenders. He now owned the port along with 400 rifles, 20,000 rounds of ammunition, a 37mm cannon and a rapidly growing army.

Sailing east, he next captured the port of Ironia and then, leaving the navy behind defeated a federal army of 800 men at the city of La Ceiba, again, due to his masterful placement of his machine guns. Now, with Bonilla and Christmas masters of the north coast, Davila's forces surrendered. Bonilla once again became president and General Christmas became Commander-in-Chief of the Honduran army, commandante of Puerto Cortes and inspector general of the entire north coast.

Amazingly, Christmas' tactical successes not only made him famous, but his use of machine guns influenced military thinkers around the world and influenced their use during World War I.

Following his political career in Honduras and lacking any fresh revolutions to fight, Christmas returned to New Orleans, where he died in 1924.

Who could have predicted all that would happen when a railroad engineer stepped down from his locomotive and picked up a rifle? **Fight on!**

Better Me Than Him

ON May 12, 1975, Cambodian Communist forces boarded and captured the *SS Mayaguez* while it was 60 miles out to sea, in international waters. The ship and its crew were taken to the island of Koh Tang 35 miles off the coast of Cambodia.

On the morning of May 15, U.S. Marines assaulted the island to free the prisoners. With the lumbering CH-53 helicopters in plain view for almost ten minutes on their approach to the island, the communists had ample time to prepare for their arrival. As the first helicopter discharged its troops, it met a fusillade of small arms fire. The big bird was mortally wounded by rocket-propelled grenades and machine gun fire. After landing its Marines, the pilot nursed the wounded bird a mile offshore before ditching. As the helicopter rolled over and began to sink, the pilot and two flight mechanics escaped, but co-pilot Lt. Karl Poulsen was trapped in the sinking aircraft by a faulty seat belt. Seeing that Poulsen hadn't gotten out, Ssgt. Elwood Rumbaugh, by no means a strong swimmer, dove into the sinking craft, released his co-pilot, pushed him to the surface and then promptly sank beneath the waves and drowned.

Sometimes there's someone more important than yourself. **Fight on!**

Time to Give Up

FOR four days in May of 1943, over 1,200 searchers had combed the Shenandoah hills of Virginia futilely looking for four year old Doris Dean. Four days earlier the girl had followed her two brothers out to milk cows. Shooed home by them, she turned and left but never arrived home, and the search was on. Police, forest rangers, Boy Scouts and hundreds of others had combed the hills as cold nights and chilling thunderstorms destroyed all hope of finding the girl alive.

Trying to be realistic, the chief ranger advised Superintendent Dixon Freeland that it was time to call off the effort. But against all advice, Freeland instructed searchers to go to the highest point and search downward one more time. On the fifth day, the little girl was found alive and returned to her family. She told her rescuers she had, "drinked the water from the leaves." Her feeble little efforts and the tenaciousness of Supt. Freeland had saved her life.

As the following poem illustrates, some saw a Greater Hand in all of this. **Fight on!**

But Doris still is living she is happy now again
The God who watched above her, took away her pain
And we will all remember as the future years go by
That it was only by the will of God, that Doris did not die.
No man will ever follow the trail this baby made.
Only the God in Heaven saw where Doris laid
Her life will have some pleasure, a part of it will be sad
But little Doris will always need, the faith her mother had.
(Ode to little Doris Dean)

Fire, Poison Gas and High Seas

ON December 21, 1942, the U. S. Navy's World War I vintage submarine *S-35*, commanded by Lt. H. S. Monroe, was running on the surface in a winter gale with hatches open to supply fresh air to the crew below. It was about 45 miles from the Japanese held island of Kiska, Alaska, in the Aleutian Islands. Suddenly, a 25 foot wave smashed the vessel, slamming Monroe into the side of the conning tower while tons of seawater poured down the hatch like a bathtub drain. Within minutes the salt water shorted electrical wiring in the control room and a fire erupted.

The crew exhausted their extinguishers to no avail. The fire found its way to the forward battery compartment and began to fill the bow with deadly chloride gas. Soon the bow was abandoned. Then fumes crept into the control room. It was then sealed as the crew retreated aft in the doomed boat. Power to control steering and the bow and stern plates failed as the fire spread through the wiring. Dead in the water in the storm-tossed sea, firemen donned smoke lungs and went forward to fight the blaze, but they couldn't get it out. Finally, Monroe and the entire crew went topside and sealed the hatches to smother the flames.

Waves and wind battered the crew as they clung desperately to lines to keep from being swept overboard. Finally, after two long, cold hours, they returned below, managed to get the engines restarted and headed for home.

Later that day the stubborn fire re-ignited, filling the boat again with deadly fumes. Again they went topside and sealed the hatches, then back down into the smoke-filled corridors to renew their journey.

Three more times they found themselves perched on the storm-tossed hull waiting for the fires to die. Finally, on Christmas Eve, *S-35* limped into port in Adak with no loss of life. **Fight on!**

One Tough Trooper

DURING the Nez Perce Indian War, Sergeant Michael McCarthy of the 1st U.S. Cavalry, proved his toughness during a raging battle on June 17, 1877.

In his haste to catch an Indian raiding party, Captain David Perry's 90 men left Fort Lapwai without an ample supply of ammunition. In White Bird Canyon, the tiny force encoutnered over 700 Indians who were well entrenched. Retreat was impossible. Capt. J. G. Trimble, who commanded Troop H, spied some high ground to his right that would command the battlefield. He sent Sgt. McCarthy with six men to hold the point.

The mass of Indians swarmed down on the troopers. Capt. Perry, in overall command, ordered a general retreat. Capt. Trimble, realizing this action would abandon McCarthy and his men, urged a renewed attack. Perry consented and the cavalrymen turned and charged into the Indians. When Sgt. McCarthy, whose men had been pouring hot fire down on the Indians, saw the renewed cavalry attack faltering, he leaped on his horse and rode down into the fray to steady the line. That done, he galloped back to his hilltop position and rejoined his small band of men.

Soon, the overwhelming number of Indians began to drive the troopers back and once again they had to retreat. They fled to a stronger position about a mile away. This left McCarthy and his men to face the wrath of over 700 Indians. The Indians quickly surrounded the tiny band of men and rushed the hill. The men shot, clubbed and fought the attacking Indians bare-handed until the men disappeared from the view of their comrades on the distant hill. Suddenly, the men saw the blue blouses of the U.S. Cavalry as they saw Sgt. McCarthy again hacking his way through the sea of red bodies, trying to lead his men to safety.

A detachment was sent to help the brave group and all but two of the seven men made it to them. But the Indians surrounded this new group and closed in for the kill. The desperate men began fighting their way back to their lines.

They say Sgt. McCarthy was everywhere. He was seen fighting Indians. He was seen steadying his men. He was seen helping a dismounted soldier. His horse was shot out from under him. He mounted another and continued leading his men back to safety. Then his second horse was shot and his men saw him disappear among the mass of Indians.

Cut off from his men, McCarthy kept his head. He dashed for a small clump of bushes along the bank of a nearby creek and crawled in as far as possible. But his boots were still visible. Nearby was a slain trooper and some squaws approached the man's body and began to mutilate it. One woman spied McCarthy's boots and headed his way. Ever so carefully the sergeant slipped out of his boots and crawled deeper into the foliage. The woman, assuming the boots were somehow abandoned in the heat of battle, took them and returned to her grisly task.

The cavalry regained their lines and departed for their fort, leaving the gallant sergeant in the midst of the Indians, not knowing he was alive.

McCarthy waited quietly for hours until he was able to crawl along the streambed. Without boots or ammunition he began his journey back, hiding by day, traveling by night, he made his way through the tall timber until, to the surprise and delight of his fellow cavalrymen, he arrived at Fort Lapwai. **Fight on!**

"Americans are like a match box. If you strike one they all go off!"

(The sultan of Sulu, 1900, watching his Moro warriors in the Philippines consistently defeated by American troopers.)

"I Didn't Have Time to Feel Sorry for Myself."

ON September 11, 2001, Muslim terrorists attacked America. Soon thereafter their compatriots in Afghanistan were scurrying from cave to cave trying to avoid the wrath of the U.S. Military under *Operation Enduring Freedom*. While taking part in that operation on December 16, 2001, Marine Sgt. Christopher Chandler stepped on a land mine near Kandahar. He lost his left leg below the knee from the explosion. Such an injury spells the end of a military career, but Sgt. Chandler, known to his friends as a "can do" type individual, didn't want out of the Marines. He fought to remain on active duty and won. But that wasn't enough for Chandler. He enrolled in airborne jump school, finishing at the top of his class. On November 10, 2003, less than two years after his injury and on the birthday of the Marine Corps, he became the only service member ever to become jump-qualified with a prosthetic leg.

Sgt. Chandler took the accomplishment in stride. "I figured I had an advantage. After all, I have one less ankle to break." **Fight on!**

Desperation at 17,500 Feet

ON May 17, 1960, two teams of climbers had just left Mt. McKinley's 20,320 foot peak and were starting back down. In the first team was 31 year old Helga Bading, who was suffering from lack of oxygen and deteriorating with dangerous quickness.

Suddenly, a four man team which was following, plunged down the side of the mountain coming to rest at the 17,500 foot level. Team leader, John Day, had broken one ankle and had severely injured the other. Paul Grew, leader of the lower party, though exhausted, scratched his way back up the mountain and stayed with Day while the more lightly injured men continued the descent to their camp. Grew also made a radio call for help to the Alaska Rescue Group. Before it was over the epic rescue would involve airplanes, helicopters and 60 rescue climbers. Two of those rescuers would die when their plane slammed into the mountain.

Helga Bading's condition was now critical in the 30 degree below zero temperatures and a climbing partner, who was a physician, despaired for her life. To survive they had to get her off the mountain quickly.

No one knew the mountain better than Brad Washburn, but he was thousands of miles across the continent in Boston. Yet, via a long distance call, he gave pilot Don Shelton exacting instructions that plopped his Piper Super Cub right down on the side of the mountain at the 14,000 foot level on May 20, higher than anyone had ever landed an airplane before. On his first daring trip he removed Bading, who would live due to his heroic efforts. On his other 17 remarkable landings, he brought in supplies for the rescue parties who were trying to reach the others 3,500 feet above.

Also setting a high altitude landing record that day was Link

Luckett when he dropped his straining Hiller helicopter in at 17,200 feet and took on John Day. But, try as it might, the tiny craft didn't have enough power to lift off the mountain with its load. Something had to be done. Daringly, Luckett had two brothers from the climbing party position themselves on each side of the small helicopter. As he pulled the throttle wide open he called for the men to lift up on the skids and "throw" the craft off the mountain. Then Luckett dove down the side of the precipice to gain airspeed before flying off with his charge.

There were still several climbers to be rescued when a vicious blizzard descended on the mountain. For 40 hours desperate men clung to the mountain as 135 mph winds tried to blow them off. Finally, the storm broke and tired, frozen men slowly ascended the mountain and retrieved the last of the climbers. It had taken nine days of determination and heroic acts but all were safely brought off the mountain. **Fight on!**

Why They Called Him "Great!"

FOLLOWING his victory over the Indian Army at the Hyphasis River, in late 326 BC, Alexander the Great attacked the city of Multan. His troops had forced their way into the city, and the Indians had retreated to the citadel. As his men hesitated to throw up their ladder (they had only two), Alexander grabbed one, threw it against the wall and dashed up against a hailstorm of Indian arrows. At the top, he beat back the defenders, climbed over onto the parapet and, with his sword flailing, killed its defenders. As he stood there alone, even more arrows rained down on him from higher walls, but his shield deflected them as his sword fought on.

Below, his men knew he must soon be hit and beckoned him to jump to safety in their arms. He did jump....the other way. His blood boiling with the rage of battle, Alexander leaped down into the citadel. Miraculously, the Macedonian landed on his feet, backed against the wall and prepared to defend himself. Frenzied Indians attacked but all fell before this one-man-army. More defenders surged forward only to fall before Alexander's flashing sword. Confused, they stood around the fearless warrior in a half-circle and did all they could to fell him.

Suddenly, an arrow slammed into Alexander's chest, piercing his left lung. At that very moment three of his men dropped down beside him, having finally scaled the wall. The Indian troops tried to overwhelm them but still Alexander's sword took its toll. Finally, Alexander staggered and fell. His men rushed forward and covered him with their shields and bodies to protect him from the missiles.

Outside, his men, mad with concern for their leader, mounted the wall like army ants and leaped into the fray. They exploded in rage and wiped out the defenders and secured their leader.

Later, in Alexander's tent, his physician hesitated to remove the arrow, fearful the Macedonian would die and all would blame him. Perceiving this, Alexander demanded, "Why are you waiting? If I have to die, why do you not at least free me from this agony as soon as possible?"

His surgeon, resolved to perform the life threatening surgery, called for men to hold Alexander down during the procedure. Alexander said they would not be needed, laid down and didn't move while the arrowhead was removed. He fully recovered. **Fight on!**

The Tale of Two Men

ON February 1, 1932, pilot, Lt. Edward Hoffman, and observer, Lt. William Cocke, left San Francisco's Crissey Army Air Field and flew right into a blinding snow storm. As their ice-covered plane lost altitude, Lt. Cocke bailed out, leaping into a driving blizzard. After landing, he trudged out through the blowing snow storm and came upon a remote ranger cabin. He spent the night there and hiked out to safety the next day.

After Cocke jumped, Hoffman continued flying until he realized his plane would not remain aloft, and he bailed out. Landing three miles from where his plane crashed, Hoffman first attempted to light a fire but gave up in the vicious snowstorm. Then, basically uninjured, he laid down, went to sleep and never woke up. It would be two months before his body was found. He was just a few feet from a trail that led to the safety of the Lake Canyon Lodge just three-quarters of a mile away. **Fight on!**

Avenging His Brother

RON Rosser joined the Army at age 17 in 1946 and was too late to see fighting in World War II. He was discharged and back home in Columbus, Ohio, by 1949. But one of his younger brothers enlisted after him and was killed in the fighting in Korea. That was too much for Rosser who promptly re-enlisted and put in for combat duty in Korea.

Arriving in the lines in Korea, he was told he would be first gunner in a mortar platoon. He promptly informed his captain that he wasn't going to a mortar platoon, he was going to the lines to engage the enemy who had killed his brother. The captain repeated his assignment to mortars. The determined soldier looked the captain in the eye and said, "Captain, I can't think of a d---- way you can stop me!"

Flabbergasted, the captain told him the only men needed on the line from his company were forward observers (FO) and radio-telephone operators (RTO). He then informed the captain he was the best FO he had ever seen. But no FO's were needed at that time. Just then word came that they had just lost an RTO. "I'm the best RTO you've ever seen," was Rosser's reply. He was now an RTO and soon after, was made a forward observer. As a forward observer he rained death on the enemy. Wounded several times, he refused treatment because he didn't want to be pulled from the line.

Then came January 12, 1952, and his Medal of Honor. Leaving their lines before dawn in -20 degree temperatures, his patrol circled behind Hill 472 to attack it from the rear at dawn.

But unknown to them, an entire battalion of Chinese Communist soldiers waited rather than the "handful" they expected.

The volume of enemy fire was horrendous and with all the officers killed or wounded, Rosser soon found himself leading the surviving 35 soldiers in one final attempt to take the hill, while five enemy machine guns raked the hillside like a scythe. Undaunted, he and a few soldiers charged straight up the hill through enemy fire. Their objective was a Chinese trenchline. A few feet from the trench, Rosser looked and saw that every man but him had been shot. He was alone. He straddled the trench and shot one Chinese soldier just as another stuck a burp gun in his back. Before he could pull the trigger, Rosser turned and killed him. Then he jumped into the trench and ran down it shooting Chinese soldiers as he came upon them.

So devastating was Rosser's one-man attack that the enemy actually sighted in a 76mm high velocity gun to eliminate him. Alone and trapped at one end of the trench, 35 Chinese Communist soldiers came running at him. Figuring death was imminent anyway, he faced them and charged, screaming wildly. They turned and ran as Rosser dropped numbers of them one-by-one. A grenade landed at his feet and Rosser dove over a dead Chinese soldier as the grenade went off, blowing the heel off one of his boots.

Now isolated and out of ammunition, Rosser ran the 40 yards back to his lines to bring up more men. On his way back to his lines, he grabbed a wounded soldier and carried him to safety.

Rosser had cleared an enemy trench, rescued a wounded soldier and returned to his lines unhurt. But he wasn't finished! He restocked his ammunition supply and gathered up more than a dozen hand grenades. Then he slung his carbine over his shoulder, took a grenade in each hand, pulled the pins and with incredible determination, started back up the hill. With grenades and rifle fire, Rosser cleared trenches and enemy bunkers.

One Chinese soldier threw a grenade and wounded Rosser in the hand. That so enraged the Columbus corporal that he chased the man down and shot him. But his pursuit had led him behind enemy lines and right into the midst of the Chinese soldiers. They swarmed at him. He tossed a phosphorus grenade into the air above a mass of Chinese soldiers. It leveled them and Rosser ran right through their ranks, shooting them as he went. He then jumped into an empty Chinese trench, out of hand grenades and ammunition. Just then a Chinese Communist soldier straddled the trench just six feet away and leveled his submachine gun at him. Rosser raised his empty carbine and pointed it at the enemy's face. For eternal seconds they looked at each other and then Rosser let out a blood-curdling scream and the enemy soldier turned and ran. Rosser leaped from the trench, grabbed another wounded American and headed back to his lines.

A third time a grenade-laden Rosser ran back up the hill and rained his deadly missiles on the enemy.

By now it had been decided by headquarters to withdraw the men back to American lines. But gathering wounded men scattered all over the hillside, directly under enemy fire, presented quite a problem.

Rosser was determined not leave anyone behind. He rounded up every man he could and made yet a fourth armed foray up the hill to retrieve their wounded comrades.

What does Rosser advise in combat? "If you ever get the enemy running, keep them running and don't give them the chance to come back at you. Don't be stupid, but don't be afraid, as there is nothing really to be afraid of." **Fight on!**

"I heard pilots express the opinion that the admirals looked upon the fliers as expendable, and I suppose they must to a certain extent, but I shall never again feel that they wouldn't do everything conceivable in their power to bring a pilot back.... It was a demonstration I shall never forget."

A dive bomber pilot from the *Enterprise*, WWII

Light Up the Night

THE final air strike of the Pacific's Marianas' campaign of World War II had to launch late in the day. This meant that the battle weary flyers would be returning to their aircraft carriers in the dark. The pilots, low on fuel, would have to somehow locate their mother ships in the inky Pacific darkness while those same ships cruised on in blackout conditions. This was to prevent becoming the target of a prowling Japanese submarine.

As the wandering pilots chattered among themselves in the blackness, unable to find their ships and contemplating the hopelessness of surviving a nighttime ditching in the rough Pacific water, Vice Admiral, Marc A. Mitsher, made a benevolent but dangerous decision. He ordered all of the aircraft carriers to turn on their lights.

Before the bewildered pilots eyes the pitch blackness came alive in light. Suddenly ships appeared where only blackness had been. Star shells fired from destroyers attracted many flyers' attention. Searchlights guided them to the carriers. And there were those beautiful red lights marking the flight decks. There were even individual sailors shining flashlights into the night. Anything to help the helpless flyers come home.

And home they came! Plane after plane roared out of the darkness to be grabbed from the air and then be quickly pushed aside and parked. The pilots would never forget how they were not abandoned by the fleet. **Fight on!**

Treachery Never Pays

DURING the Argonne offensive of September 1918, Lt. Dwite Schaffner of the U.S. Army had crawled out and silenced a German machine gun nest with his pistol.

In his absence, a group of German soldiers approached his platoon with their hands raised calling out, "Kamerad!" The battle-weary doughboys welcomed the surrender and joyously strode out to receive the surrendering soldiers' weapons. It was a trick. Suddenly other Germans in hiding opened fire, devastating the exposed Americans.

Lt. Schaffner saw the treachery from the machine gun position he'd just taken. Enraged by the deceit, Schaffner charged the Germans with his pistol and hand grenades. His pistol empty, he took it by the barrel and beat several Germans to death with the butt. The remaining Germans retreated. Schaffner's indignation had saved his men. **Fight on!**

A One Night Stand

DURING the Boxer Rebellion of China in 1900, numerous foreigners were butchered by the Buddhist Patriotic League of Boxers. These radicals, driven by hatred and racism, surrounded the legations of foreign powers and attempted to overrun them and kill all within. Until a relief force made up of troops from Japan, Russia, England, Germany, France, Austria, Italy and the United States could relieve them, the meager guard force would have to hold out, alone.

On July 14, one month before the relief force arrived, Private Daniel Daly provided a little relief of his own. On that day the Boxers had breached the flimsy barricade and were in danger of overrunning the American legation. To give the haggard defenders time to repair their defenses, Pvt. Daly crawled out on top of the Tartar wall. There, alone, far from support or rescue, he fired on the Boxers, killing many of the "immortals" outright. All night long his fire held the Boxers back while the barricade was being repaired.

It was dark, and Pvt. Daly was too preoccupied to see several Boxers quietly scaling the wall. Suddenly they leaped to their feet and, wielding swords, charged the lone Marine screaming, "Sha! Sha!" (Kill! Kill!) With no time to chamber a round, Daly used both his bayonet and rifle butt to clear the wall of intruders. By morning the breached barricade was repaired, the legation was saved and the ground beneath Pvt. Daly was littered with the bodies of the "immortal" Boxers. Daly won the Medal of Honor, one of two he was to be awarded. **Fight on!**

7 Now when Ebed-melech the Ethiopian, one of the eunuchs which was in the king's house, heard that they had put Jeremiah in the dungeon; the king then sitting in the gate of Benjamin;

8 Ebed-melech went forth out of the king's house, and spake to the king, saying,

9 My lord the king, these men have done evil in all that they have done to Jeremiah the prophet, whom they have cast into the dungeon; and he is like to die for hunger in the place where he is: for there is no more bread in the city.

Jeremiah 38:7-9

Black, Brave & Stubborn

FOUR young Union prisoners-of-war were committed to gruesome solitary confinement in the Southern prison known as the "Warehouse Prison." Before their confinement in solitary, their existence had been difficult enough. Three hundred and seventy-eight stinking, dirty, underfed men were jammed into this old tobacco warehouse. Food was so scarce that the prisoners received only a weak soup, mostly made of water, and a crust of bread.

But, unbelievably, these four men, in their dark little cell, found themselves well fed. They had plenty of bread and even alittle meat. How could this be? Every night a silent figure stole through the shadows, knelt at their door and slipped the men food, even though it was against the rules.

One day guards called the four out of their cell. Before them stood a black man, bound. This was their mysterious benefactor. Now he would pay for his kindness. The man's shirt was stripped off, he was bound to a bench and then beaten bloody before the men. Then salt was rubbed into his wounds. He was released, thrown his shirt and ordered back to work as the horrified Union soldiers were returned to their confinement.

Late that night, as the men pondered the day's happenings and the slave's fate, they heard a noise outside their door. Then a faithful black hand pushed bread and meat in to the men. When begged, for his own good, to leave and not return, a quiet steady voice was heard in response, "It's all I can do mar'se, it's all I can do." **Fight on!**

An Icy Tomb

IN December of 1936 Fred Easley and two fellow prospectors were slowly making their way toward a mine in Lucky Chance Mountain when a sudden avalanche buried them. The snow was wet and heavy. Fred was pinned face down beneath its surface. He knew he would die here but thoughts of the grief it would bring to his mother motivated him to try to escape his icy tomb. He slowly worked his right hand free and then his right leg. He clawed at the snow with his hand and then forced it behind him with his foot. Finally he saw a glimmer of light, tore at it and broke a small hole open on the surface. Still trapped, he called out and was thankfully rewarded by a response from his friends who were slowly digging themselves out. "We'll have you out in a little while," they called. Just then a second, larger avalanche plowed into the group. It tumbled his friends far down the mountain while it buried Fred beneath 21 feet of hard wet snow. Unbeknownst to Fred, his friends finally freed themselves but, frostbitten, injured and unsure of where he was buried, they stumbled off to get help to find Fred's body.

Fred was now entombed in frigid darkness listening to the sounds of the snow as it settled and packed even harder. But he refused to give up. He managed to retrieve some food from the lunch pail he was carrying to renew his strength. Then he resumed his digging.

Day turned into night, but still he dug, inching forward, afraid that if he slept he would never awake again.

For two whole days he dug and crawled, inch by inch.

Freezing, growing weaker, he continued his struggle against the snow, dragging snow behind him and pushing himself a few inches forward.

He was dozing, hallucinating and near exhaustion. Still he fought on, turning his tomb into a tunnel. He had exhausted his strength when he heard the sound of digging. He cried out to anyone who could hear him. Suddenly he heard a loud crunch and a shovel appeared before his face. For fifty-two hours he had dug and dragged himself for 15 feet beneath the snow to meet rescuers who thought they would only find a body. They did. But this one was warm! **Fight on!**

Aggressive to the End

A small convoy of about 30 Army reservists in Iraq in 2004 were attacked by over 200 Muslims. They held their own for two hours at which time they were in danger of running out of ammunition. A call for help brought a pair of AH-64 Apache attack helicopters. One was piloted by Chief Warrant Officer Chuck Fortenberry. CWO Fortenberry, a born-again Christian and nineteen-year Army veteran, had passed on the opportunity for an "early out" and chose deployment to Iraq. His father said he did it because, "He felt he could save lives."

CWO Fortenberry roared in on the Muslim terrorists while his gunner CWO Shane Colton blasted away at their positions. The sleek helicopter made pass after pass. Then suddenly a shoulder-launched surface-to-air missile tore into the ship's tail. Because helicopters do not glide, Fortenberry had only a few seconds for an emergency landing. He spied a group of Iraqis and, rather than seek safety, turned into them while Colton hammered away to relieve the ground troops. After that pass, the helicopter simply quit flying, plummeted to earth and exploded.

CWO Fortenberry's selflessness had achieved exactly what he had wanted. He had saved lives - at the expense of his own. **Fight on!**

Mad Grab at Life!

ON July 4, 1944, two World War II B-24 bombers collided in midair and 2nd Lt. George B. Smallfield, pilot of one of the aircraft, was pitched out of his airplane at 10,000 feet without a parachute. As he fell to certain death, Lt. Smallfield spied a parachute falling to earth right beside him. He had one chance at survival. The desperate flyer grasped at the chute, and, still falling, quickly donned it and pulled the rip cord. He was the only man from his aircraft to survive. **Fight on!**

In God is my salvation and my glory: the rock of my strength, and my refuge, is in God.

Trust in him at all times; ye people, pour out your heart before him: God is a refuge for us. Selah.

Psalm 62:7-8

The Ultimate Emergency Locator Transmitter

PILOT and former pastor, Mike Carlton, was ferrying a Cessna 180 from Anchorage to McGrath, Alaska, on March 12, 1988, when he suddenly flew into a devastating wind shear. The invisible wind on the otherwise clear day bounced the little plane all over the sky. It blew him toward a mountain ridge line. Carlton banked away from the onrushing mountainside but the wind carried his light aircraft right into it. Dazed by the impact, Carlton was taking stock of his situation and good fortune of not having any broken bones when the angry wind lifted the wingless fuselage and tossed it over the ridge. The demolished aircraft finally stopped tumbling. When Carlton came to he realized he still had no broken bones or serious injuries. Many snow covered miles from civilization, he settled in as best he could to await rescue, hoping his Emergency Locator Transmitter had activated, which would lead rescuers right to him. It hadn't. The temperature was near zero.

After a cold, sleepless, foodless night, Carlton's hopes sunk. The day was heavily overcast. For five days he waited for it to clear as he heard airplanes above him searching in vain through the clouds.

After five days of futile waiting, Carlton decided that he would try walking out. He would rather die doing something than just sitting there freezing. But strange things were happening that he knew nothing about.

That morning, Jerry Olson, a Christian pilot who had found many a downed flyer, awoke with an overwhelming burden to go help in the search. After work that evening, he left a note to his supervisor that he was taking a few days off to do just that. But when he arrived home he got an unexpected call from one of Carlton's friends and fellow preacher, Jim Brenn. Brenn told him, "Jerry, the Lord spoke to me to find Mike. Let's go find him and bring this man home."

The next day was clear and the two men searched the grid assigned to them by the rescue coordinators but both men knew in their hearts that Carlton wasn't in their assigned area.

Meanwhile, Carlton had exited his wrecked plane and started off to rescue himself. After about six arduous hours of struggling through the deep snow, he realized what seven days in sub-zero weather with no food had done to him. The six hours had netted him a total distance of two miles.

Finished with their assigned area, Olson and Brenn decided to search an area 20 miles west. Olson pointed his Super Cub into the first canyon. Suddenly he felt strange. He sensed their goal was near. Before he could put his thoughts to words, Brenn smacked him on the shoulder from the rear seat and exclaimed, "He's here. Close by. I know he's here."

Struggling through the seventh hour of what he thought would be the last walk he took, Carlton suddenly heard the rhythmic beat of an airplane engine. He looked up into the eyes of Jerry Olson as Olson banked hard to port and then wagged his wings. They'd found him!

Now to retrieve the endangered pilot. Daylight was slipping away. In his fragile condition Carlton wouldn't survive a night in the open. Plus, Olson and Brenn had spotted a pack of wolves nearby who were sure to get the stranded pilot's scent.

The Piper Cub is a remarkable airplane. Lightweight and of sturdy construction with gobs of lift, it begs to fly. This author once saw a lone pilot nose his Cub into the wind, release the brakes and take off in about 100 feet. It didn't take off so much as simply lift up into the sky. In a stiff wind they were also famous for some very short field landings.

Jerry Olson's plane was an up-powered Super Cub. Long on power and short on weight, the tandem seat aircraft could put down and take off in areas too small for anything but a helicopter. But even here there was no place to safely land and pick up the downed pilot in the receding daylight. But one topographic feature caught the veteran pilot's eye. A small ledge about 200 feet long with a 150 foot cliff at its end. After calling Rescue to announce their discovery, Olson swung into the wind. He planned to land and exchange Brenn for Carlton and take off. Brenn, with the advantage of being fresh and having snow shoes, would then hike down to a spot where another soon to be arriving plane could land and pick him up.

Olson crossed the threshold of this postage stamp landing spot. He reduced power and pulled the nose up forcing the tail down into the four foot deep snow which acted like an anchor and brought the plane to a stop less than 50 feet.

Two hundred feet farther down the slope Mike Carlton knew he was saved. But when he saw Jerry Olson he didn't understand. He had distinctly felt the Lord inform him, "I will send a friend to get you." But he and Olson had never met. "Who are you?" he asked. Before Olson could answer, Mike Carlton's old friend, Jim Brenn, leaned forward from the backseat and called out. A few minutes later the two men had hiked down to the exhausted pilot. With tears frozen on his ashen face, Mike Carlton embraced his old friend.

It took a half an hour for the two men to help the hypothermic, literally half-frozen man to the ledge where they'd left their plane. Now another problem arose. The drag from the deep snow would not allow Jerry to get up enough airspeed to take off in the short distance in front of his plane, and there was no way to turn the plane around to utilize the full length of the ledge for takeoff. There was only one thing to do - they would have to jump off the cliff - with the airplane!

Olson fired up his engine, pulled full throttle and taxied right over the cliff and out of sight of the horrified Brenn, left standing on their makeshift landing strip. The small aircraft dove straight down. It had about 100 feet to gain both speed and lift. Suddenly, to his heartfelt relief, Brenn saw the top of the small airplane as it clawed its way into the air with its precious cargo.

Mike Carlton's Emergency Locator Transmitter never activated. Would be rescuers were searching in the wrong area. He would never have been found if the *Ultimate* Emergency Locator Transmitter had not alerted two fellow Christians and directed them right to their objective. **Pray on!**

Brown vs. Brown

NO one picks a fight with a bear, but they happen just the same. Now, slashed and bitten in a nose-to-nose fight with an Alaskan brown bear, Greg Brown stood there with his intestines hanging out of a gash to his abdomen. But, there was still enough fight left in him to take care of this adversary and then some. In the fleeting moments between attacks, Brown snatched up his rifle, too damaged by the encounter to fire, and clubbed his assailant into a candidate for a bear skin rug.

Now, what to do about all this rearranged plumbing. No problem. The dauntless warrior retrieved a sail mending needle and some nylon line, pushed everything in to about where it looked right and sewed himself up. Then he hauled himself off to the hospital where he completely recovered. Could there have been any doubt? **Fight on!**

With a Submarine on His Back

THE submarine *S-51* had sunk off the coast of New England in over 130 feet of water. In order to raise it, deep sea divers had secured cables around the bow & stern but needed to place another amidships. Problem. *S-51* had settled into the clay bottom. Divers wearing bulky, hard hat diving suits would have to burrow a tunnel under the crippled boat using a high pressure water hose. Down, and then under, following the sub's contour, a diver would blow the tough clay away and then, head first, crawl in and push the tunnel farther.

Diver Francis Smith was now in the tunnel. Laying on his stomach in pitch blackness, with the hull of the sub against his back and not enough room to turn around, he was extending the tunnel which swirled with silt-filled water. Sea water slowly seeped into his suit as he worked in the horizontal position. Then, almost 20 feet down and under the sub, Smith felt the sea bottom give way. He felt the clay settle onto his legs as it filled the tunnel. He was trapped in a lightless hole, under water, with an entire submarine, which was soon to be his tombstone, on his back. Panic filled his very being. It had taken two weeks to extend the tunnel to its present length, meaning it would take that long for divers to reach Smith.

Topside began to dispatch help but no one thought Smith could be saved. Over the microphone in his copper helmet, he told them to keep the water pumping. If he was going to get out, he would have to get himself out. Smith couldn't turn around, so he turned the hose nozzle around and pushed it backwards until he could grip it between his bulky diving boots. Then he slowly crawled backwards, blowing the clay out as he went. After an eternity he emerged from the tunnel onto the ocean floor. The amazing diver sat on the sea floor for a few minutes to collect himself. Then he crawled back into the blackness of the tunnel to continue working! **Fight on!**

Where's the Kitchen Sink?

IN November of 1864 two soldiers had just finished some official business at Fort Zarah in Kansas and were returning to Fort Riley, Kansas, by wagon. About five miles after leaving the fort, Captain Henry Booth, accompanied by a Lieutenant Hallowell, were set upon by nearly 30 Indians on horseback. The soldiers turned the wagon around and headed back to Fort Zarah at top speed with the howling Indians in pursuit, gaining on them every second.

Lt. Hallowell took the reins while Captain Booth went back into the wagon and armed himself with one of three revolvers they had and returned fire on the hostiles who, for the most part, were armed with spears and bows and arrows. Soon the Indians were galloping along both sides of the wagon, pelting it with arrows.

Booth heard Hallowell cry that he'd been hit and turned to see an arrow sticking out of his head above the right ear. He rushed forward and plucked it out, while Hallowell, too scared to be unconscious, kept driving like Jehu.

Booth returned to his place only to hear Hallowell cry out again, this time with an arrow lodged above his left ear. He removed that one also and, assured by Hallowell that he was all right, again returned to the back of the wagon. Just then the jostling wagon hit a rut and bounded into the air pitching Booth out the back. The quick-reacting officer hung onto the wagon and climbed back in, but he had dropped his pistol.

Booth grabbed the second revolver and moved up front and shot Indians as they tried to launch arrows at Hallowell.

Soon that one was empty! Two Indians closed in. While Hallowell beat one back with his whip, Booth pointed his empty pistol at the other and yelled, "Bang!" The Indian ducked and pulled away from the wagon. Another took his place who had seen the exchange, and Booth's second "Bang!" did not produce the desired effect. As he closed in, Booth threw the gun at him and hit him, causing him to lose both his bow and his desire to fight. Suddenly Hallowell cried out again as a third arrow lodged in his left shoulder. Then another struck his right hand and a third buried itself in Booth's shoulder.

Still full of fight, Booth armed himself with the third revolver only to find it empty. With no time to load it, it soon became a missile driving off another potential killer. Searching for any other weapons, Booth came up with the two mens' sabers. Out of their scabbards they came. Too short to reach their enemy, the four items did indeed reach the enemy as Booth hurled them with an arm that in another time and another place would have handed him a job in the Major Leagues.

They were closing on the fort now, but still the Indians attempted to stop them. Booth looked through the wagon for what he could throw at them next. All he found were the grips each man had containing their clothes. The next Indian to close on the wagon received his own gift luggage upside his head and quit the fight. Out went the other as the men finally reached the safety of the fort's main gate.

Remarkably, both men survived. Booth went on to serve in the Kansas Legislature and even became the Speaker of the House from 1889 to 1890. **Fight on!**

"The American fighting man has his failings. He is prone to many regrettable errors. But the sagacious enemy will never let him get close enough to see whom he is attacking. When he has seen the enemy, the American regular will come on in. To stop him you must kill him. And when he is properly trained and has somebody to say "Come on!" to him, he will stand as much killing as anybody on earth."

Unknown

Ferocity vs. Numbers

WHEREVER America goes, people's lives improve. Schools and hospitals are built. Roads and communications improve, and the lives of the citizenry benefit. But to those who desire control over people, these improvements are a threat to their plans.

In 1911, although the lives of Filipinos were benefitting from the American presence, rebels began murdering their own Filipino brethren in an attempt to stop progress. On September 24, a shore party of sailors from the *USS Pampang* was searching for outlaws on the island of Basilan. A lieutenant and a small group of sailors were investigating a deserted village when they were ambushed by rebel Moro tribesmen. The lieutenant was killed, and several sailors were wounded. Then the Moros ran out to hack the survivors to death with their machetes. Three sailors were nearby and charged into the group like enraged bull dogs. They fired at the mob of Moros until they were out of ammunition then took their rifles by the barrels and clubbed their enemies. The Moros, stunned by the intensity of the Americans' attack, retreated, and the wounded sailors were taken back to the ship. **Fight on!**

One Man's Fury

FOR twelve bloody days, Private Clarence B. Craft of the 96th Army Division had watched his fellow soldiers die. They were trying to take Hen Hill on the island of Okinawa. The hill was so steep and the Japanese so well entrenched that even attacks of strength had ended in bloody failure. Many times Japanese defenders would pull the pins on their hand grenades and simply let them roll down the hill into the charging Americans.

But today Pvt. Craft had had enough. After his six-man patrol was cut to ribbons, the 18 year old Californian snapped. He stood up and charged up the hill alone, he lobbed hand grenades into machine gun nests as he passed and kept going. The men of his company formed a "bucket brigade" and passed Craft a steady stream of hand grenades. In three minutes, Craft was on top of the hill. Japanese soldiers scrambled to escape this fighting machine, but Craft chased after them. He reached the enemy's main trench and emptied his rifle into it and then silenced a final machine gun emplacement with a grenade.

As American troops swarmed the hill, the Japanese fled to a nearby cave. Craft got a satchel charge and heaved it inside. It failed to go off. The defiant young private charged into the cave and retrieved the charge. He relit it and again tossed it into the cave. A deafening explosion spelled the end of enemy resistance on Hen Hill. And with the fall of Hen Hill, the Japanese line crumbled, all because one soldier had had enough. **Fight on!**

Stubborn Americans

THE "Lost Battalion" of World War I was neither lost nor a true battalion. The 308th Infantry Battalion was far under strength when it took part in an Allied attack into the Argonne Forest on October 2, 1918. The 308th was successful in reaching its objective, the ruins of the old Charlevaux mill, but their French flank support failed and withdrew. The 675 men of the 308th was far beyond Allied lines. German troops quickly moved in behind the men and cut them off. They were surrounded and marked for destruction. The Germans hammered the Army troop with machine guns, mortars and hand grenades. If that wasn't enough, Allied artillery misjudged their location and fired into the desperate men, killing and wounding scores. For five horrific days the tenacious Americans hung on. Now, low on food, ammunition and medical supplies, the Germans sent a message honorably calling for their surrender. The commanding officer, Major Charles W. Whittlesey, refused the offer. Then the defiant Americans challenged their German foe, "Come and get us!" The stunned German commander ordered an all-out attack using flame throwers against the Americans. With searing tongues of fire they assaulted the Americans. But Major Whittlesey ordered a counterattack. In a brutal battle, using pistols, bayonets and their bare hands, the weary Americans broke the German attack.

Finally a relief force fought its way to the 195 survivors. Offered a ride out of the area in a command car, Major Whittlesey declined, and, blood-stained and battered, led his men out on foot. **Fight on!**

Five Years Stranded on an Island

ON November 25, 1809, the brig, *Navigator*, struck a submerged iceberg (a "growler") in the North Atlantic and promptly sank. The crew hastened into the vessel's whaleboat with just the clothes on their backs.

Seven weeks of slowly drifting south found only two men left alive: Jim Nicholl and Dan Foss. Now, deep in the South Atlantic, their tiny boat drifted toward a small island. It was caught in the surf, capsized and Nicholl was drowned.

Dan Foss's new island home was only a half-mile wide and three-quarters of a mile long. It was completely barren of animal life, fresh water or even so much as a blade of grass. Foss began to panic as he realized the hopelessness of his plight. But then he gathered his wits about him and determined to make the best of his stay. "Why, I might as well accept what is going to happen," he said to himself. "If I am going to spend the rest of my life here and never be rescued, or if I am going to die of hunger or thirst within a few days– well, there isn't much I can do about it. And it won't make it any better to get panicky."

The days passed and Foss was slowly dying. Then one day he heard the barking of a seal. He stole up to where it was, gripped his knife and leapt upon the unsuspecting animal. He ate his fill and cut the rest in strips of seal jerky. Strengthened, Foss now heard the barking of numerous seals. With oar in hand, he rushed through them, killing seals for over three hours. That night he began dressing out 125 seals. By the time he finished, he had almost 10,000 pounds of seal meat drying in the sun.

Then came the rain. During a week long squall, Foss managed to store nearly 200 gallons of fresh water in cavities in rock surfaces, which he protected from evaporation and salt spray by placing flat stones over the small pools.

Next Foss attached his shirt to the oar and erected it on a high rock outcropping like a flag pole hoping it would be seen by a passing ship.

A year passed. Then two. During his third year he sighted a ship but it passed by without seeing him. Meanwhile, his groceries were faithfully delivered to him. A violent gale replenished his water supply and scattered fish, like manna, all over the island. Then a whale washed ashore, still wearing the harpoon of a whaler who was more successful then he knew.

Year three passed, then four. It was five years before Daniel Foss awoke to see a ship anchored off shore and a whaleboat rowing his way. But the boat held back beyond the same violent surf that had claimed Jim Nicholl five years earlier. Overcome with the fear that his long-awaited rescue would be thwarted, Foss grabbed his oar, ran to the beach and plunged in. Swimming for all he was worth, he fought free of the treacherous current and was taken aboard the *Neptune*, flying the American flag. He was landed at New Bedford, Massachusetts, and moved to Elkhurst, N.J.

Years later, asked why he had chosen to dwell so far from the sea, he said, "I'll tell you. Here I have no view of the sea. After five years alone looking at the ocean, why I've seen enough of it to last the rest of my life! I'm staying right here in Elkhurst!"

The man, whose survival seemed impossible, had survived over five years on a barren island, finally died of old age in a land-locked town, all because he had chosen not to give up. **Fight on!**

Brain Surgery at 14,000 Feet

AS four climbers descended 14,256 foot Longs Peak in the Rocky Mountains on January 27, 1968, one of them slipped and slid uncontrollably down an icy slope and smashed into a large rock crushing the front of his skull. Miraculously, he still had a pulse when the rest of his party got to him. The wind was 50 mph, the temperature near zero and headed downward with the fast fading day. The man was in great danger of dying.

One of the team went for help and, amazingly, found a doctor who returned with him while rescue plans swung into action. Eight hours later the first two of many rescuers arrived. One of them was a doctor who started an IV. The man's injury would have to be stabilized before he was lowered down the peak. The doctor, Sam Luce, used his forceps to grasp the caved-in frontal skull and eased it out, away from the brain. There were also fractures to the man's right temple, right eye and the base of the skull. Working in a tiny rock cabin, used as a shelter for climbers, Dr. Luce did what he could to stabilize the climber.

Other rescue team members arrived and fought eight more hours through a blizzard to get the man down to safety. He lived. **Fight on!**

Loyalty

ON April 11, 1944, Lt. Edward Michael was piloting his B-17 on a bombing raid over Germany. German fighters scored numerous hits on Michael's airplane. One cannon shell exploded in the cockpit ripping open Lt. Michael's right thigh and knocking out his co-pilot. Hydraulic lines for the flight controls were ruptured and a fire started in the bomb bay which was loaded with incendiary bombs. The flaming "Fortress" fell 3,000 feet. Lt. Michael pulled the burning craft out of its dive and gave the order to bail out. Only seven of the ten man crew obeyed. Lt. Michael and his co-pilot were still aboard. So was the bombardier whose parachute had been riddled and was useless. Rather than jump and leave his two crewmen to their fate, Michael declared, "All right. We'll try to make it down." Easier said than done.

For an hour the wounded plane was hammered by German fighters but still it flew on, finally shaking its pursuers in a cloud bank. Emerging from the clouds, the airplane was then subjected to a jarring flak barrage. But it flew on.

The co-pilot revived, giving Lt. Michael the opportunity to pass out. Coming to over the English Channel, the grievously wounded pilot brought his battered ship in for a landing, saving all three of their lives. **Fight on!**

You First

DURING the Civil War Battle of Mobile Bay, the Union monitor, *Tecumseh*, struck a mine, blowing a hole in her that was more than 20 feet square. The damage caused the ungainly vessel to immediately capsize and plunge to the bottom. Only ten men of the crew of 120 lived. They did so because they escaped in those frantic seconds before the boat turned-turtle.

In the pilothouse, Commander Tunis A.M. Craven made for the small opening, only big enough for one man at a time, that would allow him to escape the rapidly sinking ship. Then the pilot grabbed his leg and cried, "Let me go first, Captain, for God's sake; I have five little children."

Without hesitation, the noble captain stepped back, motioned to the passage and said, "Go on, sir."

The pilot escaped. The captain did not. **Fight on!**

Ever the Fighter

IN 1901, as the United States was stringing the first telegraph line between Fairbanks and Valdez, Alaska, a spunky young Army lieutenant and a local man were sent out in the dead of winter to survey the route. The two intrepid pioneers traveled as lightly as possible and didn't even have a tent packed onto their dog sleds. At night they simply dug a hole in the deep snow, started a fire and slept through the minus 60 degree nights.

One day, as they crossed a river, the ice gave way and dog teams, sleds and men plunged into the frigid water. They struggled out, but their clothing quickly began to freeze. Their survival depended on lighting a fire immediately. Two ax handles quickly broke as they tried to cut wood from a dead tree. But the lieutenant had thoughtfully brought along candles and had hidden matches in a shotgun shell to keep them dry. Soon the heat from the candles warmed their hands enough to assault the tree with a spare ax, and they got a fire going.

The next morning, the dauntless duo continued on, finding the body of a mail carrier who had frozen to death the previous night after an accident similar to theirs. They dutifully retrieved the mail and took it with them for delivery upon their arrival.

Their job was finished. Emmet, the local man, returned home, while the lieutenant continued his military career, finally rising to the rank of Brigadier General. He remained ever the fighter. A quarter of a century later, as General Billy Mitchell, he fought ardently for an independent air force. **Fight on!**

1 Now it came to pass upon a day, that Jonathan the son of Saul said unto the young man that bare his armour, Come, and let us go over to the Philistines' garrison, that is on the other side. But he told not his father.
2 And Saul tarried in the uttermost part of Gibeah under a pomegranate tree which is in Migron: and the people that were with him were about six hundred men;
3 And Ahiah, the son of Ahitub, Ichabod's brother, the son of Phinehas, the son of Eli, the LORD's priest in Shiloh, wearing an ephod. And the people knew not that Jonathan was gone.
4 And between the passages, by which Jonathan sought to go over unto the Philistines' garrison, there was a sharp rock on the one side, and a sharp rock on the other side: and the name of the one was Bozez, and the name of the other Seneh.
5 The forefront of the one was situate northward over against Michmash, and the other southward over against Gibeah.
6 And Jonathan said to the young man that bare his armour, Come, and let us go over unto the garrison of these uncircumcised: it may be that the LORD will work for us: for there is no restraint to the LORD to save by many or by few.
7 And his armourbearer said unto him, Do all that is in thine heart: turn thee; behold, I am with thee according to thy heart.
8 Then said Jonathan, Behold, we will pass over unto these men, and we will discover ourselves unto them.
9 If they say thus unto us, Tarry until we come to you; then we will stand still in our place, and will not go up unto them.
10 But if they say thus, Come up unto us; then we will go up: for the LORD hath delivered them into our hand: and this shall be a sign unto us.
11 And both of them discovered themselves unto the garrison of the Philistines: and the Philistines said, Behold, the Hebrews come forth out of the holes where they had hid themselves.
12 And the men of the garrison answered Jonathan and his armourbearer, and said, Come up to us, and we will shew you a thing. And Jonathan said unto his armourbearer, Come up after me: for the LORD hath delivered them into the hand of Israel.
13 And Jonathan climbed up upon his hands and upon his feet, and his armourbearer after him: and they fell before Jonathan; and his armourbearer slew after him.
14 And that first slaughter, which Jonathan and his armourbearer made, was about twenty men, within as it were an half acre of land, which a yoke of oxen might plow.

1 Samuel 14:1-14

The Courage of One Man

SAUL, the first king of Israel, was famous as a man of indecision. During one of Israel's many wars with their mortal enemies, the Philistines, he is reported to have lounged indecisively in Migron (1 Samuel 14:2). This indecision was too much for his son, Jonathan, who figured, "If we've come to go to war then let's go to war and stop wasting time." One morning he woke his armorbearer and told him that they were going to attack the Philistines at Michmash, alone. In one of history's greatest displays of pure loyalty, the young armorbearer considered the impossibility of the task but answered only, "Do all that is in thine heart: turn thee; behold, I am with thee according to thy heart." And off they went to attack the entire Philistine army!

The land between them and the Philistines had two prominent rock outcroppings, one situated to the north by Michmash, and the other to the south by Gibeah. Above the plain was a small plateau about half an acre in size where the Philistines had an outpost. The intrepid warriors revealed themselves to the Philistines on the plateau who boisterously challenged them to come up and fight. The two men climbed up hand-over-hand and reached the top. Once there, Jonathan went to work. Philistines dropped all around him while his armorbearer followed behind, finishing the job. The battle alarmed the main Philistine camp which fled. Other Jews joined in the conflict, resulting in a rout and slaughter of their enemies.

Victory had been secured by the courage of one man and the loyalty of another. **Fight on!**

The Knowledge of One Man

THREE thousand years had passed since Jonathan's great victory over the Philistines. Now, in 1917, two armies again faced each other across the valley of Michmash.

After the British took Jerusalem they were scheduled to attack the Turks at Michmash. It would be a frontal attack across the open valley directly under the Turkish guns. High casualties were expected.

That night a British soldier, a Christian and Bible reader, recalled reading about Michmash in his Bible, in 1 Samuel 14 where Jonathan and his armorbearer had attacked and defeated the Philistines. He read about the two pillars and the flat spot of ground "which a yoke of oxen might plow." He told his commanding officer about the Bible passage. Land doesn't change much. If the pillars were there three thousand years ago they should still be there. He sent out scouts and they found the pillars and the flat ground. Next, he initiated a surprise attack on the Turks that were up on the plateau. Just as the Philistines before them, the startled Turks panicked, causing a general Turkish retreat. The British marched across the valley and took up their abandoned positions. Thousands of lives had been saved all because one soldier knew his Bible. **Read On!**

> Through God we shall do valiantly:
> for he it is that shall
> tread down our enemies.
>
> *Psalm 108:13*

Commander Gilmore's Capture

THE Philippine Insurrection took place in 1898-1900 just following the Spanish-American War. On April 12, 1899, Lieutenant Commander James C. Gilmore and seventeen men from the *USS Yorktown* were attacked while in a small boat on a river near Baler Bay in eastern Luzon. From a cliff above the river scores of Filipino insurgents fired down into the little boat. Although they fought back gallantly, their oars were soon shattered by the intense fire. Most of the men were too wounded to fight back and the boat was shot through and filling with water mixed with the blood of the wounded men.

The helpless craft drifted to shore where the half-naked tribesmen rushed forward, pulled them from the boat and stripped shoes, hats, coats and personal belongings from them. Then with their hands tied behind their backs, the sailors were lined up while a hasty firing squad was gathered. Rifles came up and the Americans thought about life and their families for what they thought would be their last time. Suddenly, a native officer arrived and halted the execution. They would instead be taken prisoner. Two men, mortally wounded, would not be able to make the trek. Their American commander laid them in the shade and left them some water and then had to leave them behind to die alone.

Barefoot and in critical physical shape, the prisoners trudged to an old bamboo church building and spent the night. Then they left for the other side of Luzon. Down violent rivers, over rocky outcroppings, through pounding rain they marched.

Fearful of an attempt to rescue their captives, their Filipino captors moved constantly. At one village an insurgent general who hated all Americans sought to kill them, but, again, they managed to evade that fate.

On they marched, sick, wounded, emaciated. Days turned into weeks, weeks into months. Back and forth across Luzon they went. All told, their torturous journey stretched out over 400 miles. Then in December came a change. Their Filipino captors seemed excited and anxious. Suddenly, on December 5, the men were forced to push on deeper into the jungle. There was no sleeping, no eating, only forced marching. Word was, a force of American soldiers was in the area searching for the captives. Now, whenever possible, the men would write their names on trees and rocks to help guide their rescuers.

Finally they were forced to climb a sheer cliff face using the last of their ebbing strength. At the top they all laid down. The Filipinos met together and had an agitated conference. Then one man came over and informed Commander Gilmore that he could not hope to outdistance the Americans while maintaining their prisoners. Nor could they allow them to be rescued. They were to be shot. For a third time the men confronted death. Not one cried or begged for mercy. Goodbyes were said as their Filipino executioner looked on. Finally they were ready, but he was not. He looked at Commander Gilmore and stated, "I cannot do it. I will abandon you here in the mountains. Your own troops are not far away and you will be rescued."

They were left there with nothing but the rags they were wearing. They came upon a deserted hut and a bolo and small ax. They wandered until they came to a river. They began cutting bamboo to make a raft. As they worked they became aware of a small group of armed natives who made threatening gestures and prepared to attack. But the American spirit was alive. They armed themselves with sticks and rocks and stood their ground, prepared to defend themselves. Their resolve moved the natives to forget the attack and melt into the jungle.

Back to work they went. Suddenly they heard shouts and realized the wily natives had circled around downstream and were closing in again for the attack. Weak and bleeding hands again clutched rocks and prepared to defend themselves. Staggering men drew back their feeble arms with sticks in hand prepared to not give death an easy victory. Then around a bend downstream they saw them coming, running towards them. But these men where white! And they were wearing the blue blouses and yellow bandanas of the U.S. Army! They were rescued! Tears flowed as men embraced their countrymen for the first time in eight months. The men were fed and their wounds were treated.

The force of 150 men plus the eighteen rescued captives began a trip down the river via rafts on December 18. After eleven days of being battered, capsized and losing most of their supplies they finally came upon a friendly village whose people guided them back to the American forces.

After eight months of hopeless wandering, numerous near executions, diseases, wounds, lacking food but not spirit, the intrepid men of Commander John C. Gilmore had made it back home. **Fight on!**

Courage In a Small Package

IF you has to met 22 year old Heather Swensen, in 2006, her blue eyes would have looked at you through brown contact lenses. Her light brown hair had long been dyed jet black. Was she in hiding? Sort of. Running from the law? No, just trying to keep from being killed by either Maoist rebels or the Army of Nepal where she was doing mission work. And the danger was not in her head.

Forced to flee when King Gyandendra declared martial law, she was spirited to India in an ambulance across a bridge that was destroyed soon afterwards. Then, walking covered, but unaccompanied, in Pakistan, she was abducted three times in one day, not because she was recognized as an American, (that would have gotten her killed for sure) but because she was a female traveling alone in a male dominated Muslim society. Her first escape came when a nearby friend came to her rescue. Later she was grabbed on a side street and escaped by punching her captor in the face. Then, seemingly safe, she was strong-armed into a waiting van. Rather than panic, she carefully watched for a chance to escape and found it. When the van was forced to stop at a railroad crossing, she threw the door open and bolted.

Then, she calmly waited in India for an opportunity to return to her work in Nepal. **Fight on!**

Do Something!

DURING World War II the SS were the politically correct Nazis. Like their compatriots in today's news media, or on our college campuses, they mercilessly forced their will on those they considered "lessers." For the SS it was the Jews. They murdered over six million Jews in the concentration camps they administered. Almost four million of those helpless victims died in Auschwitz. But even those gaunt, hopeless Jews in Auschwitz found a way to fight back as they awaited the ovens.

The SS had a fondness for black pullover sweaters. They demanded that the Jewish women prisoners knit them for them. Their demand was happily met. The Jewesses made sure that every sweater was delivered on time, complete with typhus-infected lice. The SS never figured out why some of their number died of the disease. **Fight on!**

The Deadly Glasses Case

A man and his wife, who were friends of Andrew Jackson, were being pursued by a mob who wanted to take the man's wife for ulterior purposes. As the man and his wife fled into his house, Jackson stepped out of the house and stood on the steps and stopped the mob. He reached into his pocket and announced, "By the eternal God, the first man that puts his foot on this step is a dead man!" Then the crowd heard the sound of Jackson cocking the pistol in his pocket. No one wanted to be dead so they dispersed.

Later, Jackson admitted, "I had no pistol, but the snap of the spectacle case deceived them." **Fight on!**

The Captain

THE Twentieth Century was still new when a Dutch brig with a crew of nine souls departed the West Indies for home. The sea was deceitfully placid, but soon a South Atlantic hurricane reached out and overwhelmed the frail vessel. The storm snapped the ship's masts, swept the decks clean and twisted the hull until sea water poured in. Some of the men sprang to the hand pumps as others tried to staunch the leaks. They survived the storm, but as their hopes soared, a second storm assured them that their boat was doomed. Devastated by the storm, they drifted aimlessly, always bending their backs on the pumps, never quite keeping ahead of the incoming water.

Then one morning a ship appeared on the horizon! They bellowed with joy. Then they sadly realized that they had not been seen. Without masts or upper works, their hulk rode so low in the water that they were hidden by the smallest swell.

The sun baked the men and the waves caked salt on them as their hulk of a ship settled ever lower in the water. Another day. Another ship sighted! Another cheer. Another heartbreak. Day after day the men watched unbelievingly as ship after ship would appear, buoy their hopes and then sail on as though part of some vast conspiracy bent on their destruction. Fresh water and rations dwindled. Days had become weeks and ships sighted were ships ignored. All the while they pumped. All the while the sea gained on them.

Finally the resolve of the men was played out. As their captain later explained, "...the men's hearts broke." They turned to the captain who had so sincerely urged them on and, without hostility or anger, simply stated that their ship was doomed and they could do no more. For the first time in weeks the pumps went unmanned as the crew laid about on the deck of what now looked more like a raft than a ship. The sea gave no respite and rushed in to finish their little ship while they waited hopelessly for it to take them. Through the night they heard the gentle lapping of the sea as it came for them. They heard the hiss of air being replaced by water in compartments beneath them.

The sun rose and with it, the resolute captain, walked the deck of the little ship he loved for what he knew would be the last time. As the disheartened men lounged, they heard the voice of their captain. "Look at the ship!" Two, then three, stood to gaze upon the sleek vessel, sails tight with wind, as it cut the waves toward them. They had been seen at last! Then as though they could not escape the Grand Conspiracy, the wind died, their would-be rescuer's sails hung limp and the hope of all but one man sank. The captain watched as two boats were lowered, but he knew it may take more time than they had to arrive. He walked over to the pumps, bent over, took the handle and struggled against the inertia of inaction. The men realized that if they were going to be saved, they would have to take part in their own rescue. One by one they joined their captain. No words were spoken, resolute glances were exchanged. And they pumped! They pumped like madmen! Then their rescuers arrived. "To the boats!" cried the captain. They sprang as one from their positions and hurled themselves to the waiting safety. Fifteen minutes later, before they even reached their rescue vessel, the captain rose majestically and without speaking pointed. All heads turned and watched as the ocean wrapped its hands around the brig and hauled it under. "Gone."

But for their resolute captain, the crew would have gone with it. **Fight on!**

"Yankee Doodle" is Ours!

WE'VE all heard the tune "Yankee Doodle." It is as much a part of United States history as the Boston Tea Party and George Washington. Like many of the country's early citizens, like most Americans, Mr. "Doodle" was born of foreign extraction and migrated to at least one other country before establishing his American citizenship.

The tune and character originated in Holland as a song sung at harvest. It was embraced as a national song. "Hans Brinker" records one verse as:

Yanker didee dudle down
Didee dudel launter.
Yankee viver voover vown,
Botermelt und taunter.

When the English navy defeated the Dutch navy, they made up mocking verses against their foes. They personified "Yankee Doodle" as shrewd and hard-headed. The tune found a new home in England where new verses were added to mock whoever was the latest target of scorn and ridicule.

When Oliver Cromwell led his army of rebels against the King's army at Oxford, he wore a hat with a ostrich feather held in place by a heavy silk "maccaroni" band. The King's supporters sang:

Yankee Doodle came to town
Riding on a pony;
Stuck a feather in his hat
And called it maccaroni.

When the Red Coats arrived at Boston in 1775 to subdue John Hancock and his "Minute Men," they taunted the Colonials with the verse:

> *Yankee Doodle came to town*
> *For to buy a firelock.*
> *We will tar and feather him,*
> *And so we will John Hancock.*

Thus they sang in contempt for the American rebels as they marched into Lexington in April to arrest Hancock and Samuel Adams, which they failed to do, and confiscate colonial arms. The two groups met at a bridge in Lexington, a shot was fired and the rest is history.

But returning to Boston, the British were harried by colonials until their journey turned into a rout. Flushed with a surprising victory, the Colonials stole the tune and verses from the English, just as the English had from the Dutch, and sang it back to them even as they sniped at them from the woods. Humiliated, the British lost all interest in the song even as the Americans adopted it as their own. So from that day to this, Americans have been known as "Yankees," the carefree waif whom you had better take seriously. "Yankee Doodle" became a citizen of the United States, even preceding "Uncle Sam." **Fight on!**

"Terrorist attacks can shake the foundations of our biggest buildings, but they cannot touch the foundation of America."
President George W. Bush, 9/11/01

"The Americans are savages. They kill everything that moves....."
From a letter taken off a dead German in the Belleau Woods, World War I

Savage Attack on Savage Attackers

DURING Gulf War II, a Marine convoy drove right into an Iraqi ambush. Machine guns, mortars and Rocket Propelled Grenades (RPG) were hammering the trapped Marines.

Lt. Brian Chontosh was commanding the Marine column. Seeing they were cut off and hopelessly outgunned, Lt. Chontosh did the only thing he could do...he attacked! Chontosh ordered his HUMVEE driver to head straight at the Iraqi machine gun nest while his own machine gunner blazed away at it. The enemy machine gun was silenced. Then he told the driver to drive directly at the Iraqi trench. There, Lt. Chontosh jumped out, as it has been said, "carrying an M-16 and a Beretta and 228 years of Marine Corps pride."

Chontosh ran down the trench line killing Iraqis until his M-16 was empty. He then pulled his Beretta automatic pistol and emptied it on them. Next he picked up a dead Iraqi's AK-47 and fired it until it was empty. He grabbed another AK and continued his attack. Finally, he picked up an enemy RPG and disposed of the remaining Iraqis.

Lt. Chontosh single-handedly cleared 200 yards of Iraqi trenchline, turned a sure defeat into a victory and saved his men. **Fight on!**

The Warrior

ON February 19, 1945, the Marines landed on Iwo Jima. The 22,000 Japanese defenders had a tunnel complex 30 to 50 feet underground. Iwo Jima was shaped like an upside-down pear with Mt. Suribachi at its tip. Company A, 28 Regiment had the goal of crossing the narrow neck of the island thus cutting Suribachi, to its left, off from the rest of the island. Climbing hills of volcanic sand, the equivalent of running up a pile of grain, the Marines were being cut to pieces by multiple crossfires on concealed enemy bunkers. The advance stalled. Then, 23 year old Corporal Tony Stein stood straight up to draw enemy fire while his fellow Marines charged forward. Then he charged a pillbox, knocking it out single-handedly. He charged another, and another, until several were neutralized, and he was out of ammunition. Stein stripped off his boots and ran to the beach for more ammo, carrying a wounded Marine with him. He made that trip eight more times, each time rescuing a wounded comrade. Finally, later in the day, he covered his platoon as it joined its company perimeter. For his action, Cpl. Stein was the first Medal of Honor winner on Iwo Jima. **Fight on!**

The "Berber Banzai"

IT happened during the Korean War. It was a frigid Korean night with temperatures well below zero. French soldiers were huddled in frigid foxholes trying to keep warm. Even while the French battalion fought to keep from freezing to death, an entire Communist Chinese division silently crept towards them across the snow. At 2 AM Chinese bugles sounded, launching the attack. The French WWII air raid siren went off alerting French troops and drowning out the enemy's bugles. A squad of about a dozen French and Algerian soldiers huddled in the foxholes waiting for the massive Chinese onslaught. When they saw them materialize out of the darkness, they didn't move a muscle. Closer came the Yellow Horde. Still the Frenchmen stayed stock still. Then, as the Chi Coms closed to within 60 feet of their line, the French troops leaped from their foxholes screaming, and dashed toward the onrushing Chinese in a madman's bayonet attack. This charge has become known as the "Berber Banzai." The Chinese saw the cold steel of French bayonets and death in French eyes. They stopped, turned and ran away faster than they'd come. The mad Frenchmen returned to their foxholes and their lighthearted banter. **Fight on!**

Fifty-four Days on the Mountain

LIEUTENANT David Steeves would never find out what happened to his T-33 jet trainer as he flew from San Francisco to Phoenix on May 9, 1957. One second he was flying peacefully along, and the next his airplane was tumbling from the sky as the cockpit filled with smoke. He remembered an explosion. Steeves punched out of the dying craft and landed in the desolate Sierra Nevada Mountains. Nothing would ever be found of the plane for the next 20 years, and then that would be only the canopy.

After landing, Lt. Steeves hobbled and slid down a snowfield. He built a fire to warm himself, spent a cold night under some pine trees and started out again the next morning, hoping to be spotted by the massive search that, he knew, the Air Force would be conducting. Moving toward the lower elevations, he staggered from pond to creek to snowbank, spending nights in whatever shelter against the freezing temperatures he could find. He had no food, but drank water from the ponds and creeks he stumbled across.

After fifteen days, Steeves survival was in doubt; he had been given up for dead. He staggered into a clearing and, looking across it, saw a newly built cabin which was used seasonally by park rangers. Stepping inside the deserted structure, he found it stocked with a small cache of food. Steeves ate and rested his purple colored ankles as a snow storm closed in. He searched for a map and found he was locked in the peaks of the Sierras in "Simpson Meadow." The nearest help was 20 miles away. Twice he started out. Twice he was beaten back by waist deep snow and raging mountain streams.

Almost a month after arriving, Steeves again started for a mountain pass that would lead to safety. As he struggled along, he suddenly encountered a woman on horseback. After fifty-four days in the wilderness, Lt. David Steeves was saved! **Fight on!**

You're Only Hopeless When You're Hopeless

ON October 14, 1943, fifteen inmates of the Jewish Sobibor concentration camp near Lublin decided they had been there long enough. With nothing to lose, they waited inside a camp tailor shop where SS troopers had their uniforms mended and pressed. As an SS man entered the shop, a shovel came down on the back of his head and he became a believer in the afterlife.

When fifteen pistols had been collected, the group rushed the gate of the inner compound and fought their way out the main gate to freedom. You are only hopeless when you're hopeless. **Fight on!**

He Helped Himself

O. Vanebo was a fisherman on a schooner the summer of 1920. The ship's anchor was hauled up by a winch on a 4½" cable. One day, the ship's captain fired up the winch's engine while Vanebo operated the winch itself. Suddenly, the ship rolled with a wave and when Vanebo threw out his hands to keep balance the fingers of his right hand got caught in the reeling cable. Bones snapped and blood squirted. Then his whole hand was reeled in and crushed. Next his wrist was mangled. Vanebo's fellow workers, transfixed by the horror of what they were witnessing, made no move to help him nor stop the winch's progress. The machine devoured his forearm next followed by his upper arm. Vanebo, seeing no one was moving, shouted to the captain, "Stop the engine! If you don't, I'm a goner." Jolted out of his trance, the skipper shut down the winch and men moved to Vanebo's aid. Slowly his shipmates unwound the cable revealing the mangled remains of what had been Vanebo's right arm. He knew what must be done if he had any hope of living. Rising to his feet he said, "Get a knife and cut those things so I can get a bandage on and check the bleeding." Again the men stood-stock still in horror. Impatiently, Vanebo grabbed a rusty old fishing knife and amputated his crushed arm just below the shoulder and tossed it overboard. He packed his bleeding stump with towels and then sat down and had a meal while the skipper hoisted the anchor and headed for port. Twelve and a half hours later the ship docked. Vanebo was hauled onto the dock where he walked to the hospital. He survived. **Fight on!**

Unstoppable Americans

WHEN the United States defeated the Spanish in 1899 in the Spanish-American War, Spain seceded its colonial territories to the victor. Thus Puerto Rico, Guam, Cuba and the Philippines fell to American influence. Immediately following that war came the Filipino Insurrection, waged by an ambitious Filipino resistance leader who didn't want to give up his power. The Filipinos, who fought with great courage and daring, were systematically defeated. The final great battle was for the city of Calumpit where over 4,000 insurgents were prepared for a bloody defense. Between them and the attacking Americans was a wide stream whose sole bridge had been partially destroyed. The attacking Americans would be cut to ribbons attempting to cross the stream under concentrated enemy fire.

But the unpredictable Americans approached the problem as only Americans would. Five men volunteered and crawled out onto the damaged bridge while Filipino bullets whizzed over their heads. Upon reaching the gap in the span, they dropped into the water, swam to shore and, using only revolvers, cleared Filipino trenches allowing the Army to cross. They took the city, losing only six killed and twelve wounded. **Fight on!**

Whodathunkit?

THE U.S. government abandoned South Vietnam in 1973. In April of 1975 the Communists invaded from the North and brutally took possession of the once free South. Hundreds of Vietnamese struggled to escape the coming bloody retribution of the Communists. Some did, some didn't. It was ugly and bloody. The Thai-Tang family made it out. Another bedraggled Vietnamese family come to the U.S. to wash dishes or wait tables in Chinese restaurants for hungry Americans who couldn't tell the difference. Early on, Hau Thai-Tang decided he didn't want to wash dishes or wait on tables. So, as can only be done in America, he entered Carnegie Mellon University. Graduating with a degree in engineering in the 1980's, he went on to earn an MBA from the University of Michigan.

The quiet, unassuming young man was approached by Proctor and Gamble and the General Electric Jet Engine Co. but turned both down, opting to go to work for Ford Motor Co.

Applying another American trait, hard work, Thai-Tang began upward movement. In the late '90's he worked on the successful Lincoln LS. In 2004 he was picked to head the Ford Special Vehicle Team.

But the work for which you might thank him the most was his design of the beautiful 2005 Mustang a car he loved since he first saw one in his native Saigon before his family's flight to the Promised Land. From refugee to the designer of one of America's most loved cars: It's only possible in America! **Fight on!**

"We had two or three yards of frozen seal's entrails left from the last seal, and on that we lunched, eating a little blubber with it. Poor Captain Hall used to say he really liked blubber. I like it a good deal better than *nothing!* To men as hungry as we, almost any thing is sweet; this that we ate frozen as hard as the ice we are on."

Testimony of one of the sailors stranded on arctic ice for five months.

Five Months Adrift in the Arctic

GEORGE Tyson was a Captain on October 15, 1872, although not *the* captain of the ship he was aboard as it sat locked in the ice near Greenland. He was part of an expedition hoping to reach the North Pole, or at least go farther North than anyone ever had. The ship, the *Polaris,* was ice bound and in danger of being crushed. The ship's captain had the men throw provisions onto the ice so they wouldn't be lost. Tyson and a party of eighteen crewmen were on the ice with the supplies when, with a crack , the ice broke and set the ship free and them adrift on an ice floe about four miles in circumference. The ship's captain never returned to rescue his men, abandoning them to the arctic water above Hudson Bay in the winter. The party consisted of nineteen people in all. There were some women and children with the two Eskimo hunters that accompanied the expedition.

The party built igloos to help them survive temperatures as low as 40degrees below zero. They killed a few seals, using the meat for food and the blubber for fuel for cooking. When all was gone they gnawed on the seal skins, hair and all. As the temperatures plummeted, the men (and women) would crawl into their igloos, seal the door against the cold and sit. In the cramped quarters they barely had room to move, so they literally sat and could do nothing more.

Once during the long arctic night, Tyson was alerted that

a polar bear was in the camp feasting on scattered seal scraps. He crept outside, but the bear saw him and attacked. He raised his rifle and squeezed the trigger to the ominous sound of "click." As the bear closed, he pulled the trigger two more times but still it failed to fire. He turned and ran for his shelter, reloaded his rifle along with two extra shells and headed back outside. They were too desperate for food to allow this opportunity to pass. The bear charged again and the intrepid Captain put a bullet in its heart and food on the table.

In late March they were assaulted by a field of icebergs that constantly rammed their ice floe, threatening to break it to pieces. A spring gale hit and broke the group's floe free of the pack ice and into the waters of the Labrador Sea. There the waves and wind began to break up their floe. So the twelve men, two women and five children piled into the one boat they had, made for six to eight men, and struggled west toward the main pack. For two days they fought snow squalls, waves and current until they finally reached the relative safety of the main pack. There they built new igloos, but an April gale and the pounding waves began breaking this floe, too, claiming several ice houses but no individuals.

On April 8 at midnight they heard a sharp crack and before anyone could react their floe split. The entire party was on one side while just one man and their precious boat were adrift on the other half. The two Eskimos took off after it and both they and the floe with the boat were soon lost from sight. Morning came and they saw the three men over half a mile away. But the boat was too heavy for the three of them to push into the water so, one-by-one, with Tyson leading the men, they paraded across scattered ice floes until they reached the boat, launched it and returned to camp.

On the 9th a gale blasted them, sending waves washing over the floe, soaking them all and filling with salt water the depressions in the floe that had held fresh drinking water from melted snow.

By the 11th of April the ice around them had frozen, but two icebergs had lodged so near that if a part of either should break off it would have smashed down onto the party.

On April 20, an alarm was sounded just before a huge wave swept over the floe, washing away their only tent, bedding, seal skins and most all else. The women and children, which had been sleeping in the boat for safety, were endangered when the continuing waves threatened to wash the boat right off the floe. Every man stood around it trying to hold it secure as the waves assaulted it. They stood there, fighting the waves from nine o'clock in the evening to seven the next morning. At times the waves lifted the boat, with the men clinging to it and washed it closer to the edge of the floe. When morning came they spied a more secure piece of ice, boarded the boat and abandoned their doomed former camp.

On April 28, after five months adrift, they saw a seal boat to the north, sailing to the southwest. They boarded their boat, hoisted their colors, and rowed to intercept it. But it never saw them and sailed on without hesitation. They landed on another ice floe for the night. Rather than being depressed at not being rescued, they tingled with anticipation at the thought that they would soon spy another ship.

The next day they saw another steamer. Into the boat they went again, chasing salvation. After an hour the ice closed them in and they were thwarted. But they refused to give up. They clambered onto a small piece of ice, scampered to the highest point and fired all of their rifles and pistols in unison three times. Across the sea they heard three shots in response and cheered as the steamer turned south toward them. All day long they watched until finally the ship turned southwest and sailed away. It couldn't reach them because of the floes of ice.

On the evening of April 30, they spied yet another steamer. Again the guns were fired. The ship turned toward them and was soon alongside their floe. The bark, *Tigress,* from conception Bay, Newfoundland, took them aboard. **Fight on!**

Hide in the Hide

IN the late Nineteenth Century, Jack Bickerdyke was crossing the prairie southeast of what is now Amarillo, Texas. He came upon a crippled buffalo, shot it and began skinning it while his horse grazed a short distance away. As he was finishing up, he thought he smelled smoke. He looked up to see a prairie fire roaring toward him. Bickerdyke panicked and ran for his horse, but his actions spooked the animal and it ran off while the fire approached rapidly. It was hopeless to think he could outrun the fire on foot. Bickerdyke was in a frenzy. Then he stopped, settled down and tried to think of what he could do. It came to him! He sprinted for the skinned buffalo carcass, quickly gutted it and climbed inside as the fire swept over him. The heat seared him and the smoke choked him but finally the fire passed by. The half-cooked, coughing man crawled out and gazed at the blackened earth around him. He filled his lungs with clear air and headed for his camp on foot. **Fight on!**

The Impossible Shot

BILL Burgess could see the bear that was attacking his hunting partner that cold October day on Kodiak Island. But what he saw from eighty yards away was just a brief glimpse of the big brown's head as it momentarily raised up clawing at the helpless man's back.

The brown bears of Kodiak Island are known for being big. Their bodies are big. Their heads are big. Their mouths are very big. But a bear's ear is not known for being big. Neither is a .270 caliber rifle when a bear needs to be stopped in a hurry. But the .270 deer rifle was all Burgess had that day and the bear's ear appearing momentarily above alder bushes eighty yards away was all the target he would be offered. It was basically impossible. But something had to be done before the enraged sow killed his partner. Burgess adjusted himself to the rhythm of the bear's movements. Up came the head and stopped for a second. Burgess took the shot. The impact of the .270 bullet slamming into the side of the beast's head tumbled the bear over in a full circle. She went down hard and didn't get back up, but she was still breathing. Burgess then circled around as rapidly as he could, put four more shots into her and then helped his friend back to camp.

Duane Christensen, the victim, got a total of five feet of stitches but came through the attack all right. His life had been saved by a friend who took an impossible shot when it was all he could do. **Fight on!**

"....the Liberties of America are the object of divine Protection."

George Washington

Blessed is the nation whose God is the LORD; and the people whom he hath chosen for his own inheritance.

Psalm 33:12

America's Best Ally

THERE is no human explanation as to why thirteen feeble colonies were able to defeat the greatest military power in the world during our War of Independence. That's because that victory was the result of more than human courage, intellect or ability. The Continental Army had an Ally far more powerful than the King of England.

On August 22, 1776, 15,000, British troops landed on Long Island and moved to cut off the 8,000 man army under Gen. George Washington. British General Howe skillfully led his men against the poorly trained and poorly equipped Americans. By August 27, he had driven the continentals back to the northern tip of Brooklyn where his next attack would finish them. The fledgling United States Army would soon be defeated, General Washington, their Commander-in-Chief, would be killed or captured and the war would be over. But for some inexplicable reason, Howe did not attack.

While Howe tarried, Washington mused and developed a desperate escape plan for his trapped army. He announced to his officers that the entire army would be evacuated to Manhattan Island by small boats that very night. His generals knew it would take a miracle to get the entire army across the mile wide East River right under the noses of the British. They were wrong. It took several miracles.

First, but not coincidentally, Washington's latest reinforcements were the men of John Glover's Massachusett's Company, men all skilled in handling small boats.

Second, a driving rain storm blew in that not only

obscured the fleeing army from British sentinels, but whose contrary winds kept the British fleet from sailing into the East River and cutting off Washington's only avenue of escape.

Throughout the night the Massachuttians quietly rowed their fellow soldiers to Manhattan's shore and then returned for more. But the storm passed, dawn was coming and several hundred men, including Washington, still needed to be evacuated. With the arrival of morning they would never make it across the river undetected.

But then came miracle number three which is best described by a man that witnessed it, Major Ben Tallmadge.

"As the dawn of the next day approached, those of us who remained in the trenches became very anxious for our own safety, and when the dawn appeared there were several regiments still on duty. At this time, a very dense fog began to rise (out of the ground and off the river), and it seemed to settle in a peculiar manner over both encampments. I recollect this peculiar providential occurrence perfectly well, and so very dense was the atmosphere that I could scarcely discern a man at six yards distance....we tarried until the sun had risen, but the fog remained as dense as ever."

As the last boat came ashore carrying General Washington, the miraculous fog lifted. The British were vexed that their prey had escaped and Washington's army would live to fight again.

How can you defeat an army whose Ally controls the weather? **Fight on!**

Just Doing His Job

PORTER Lewis William's job on the *Olympian, Number 15*, the Chicago, Milwaukee, St. Paul & Pacific Rail Road train heading west from Chicago to Tacoma, Washington, was to help the passengers on the train in whatever way he could. It was his job. It was that simple. He took it seriously.

Torrential June rains in the Miles City area of eastern Montana had weakened the trestle over Custer Creek. Near midnight on June 19, 1938, the trestle collapsed as *Number 15* was crossing it, plunging sleeping passengers into the raging water below.

Passengers in one car that was teetering on the water's edge, couldn't get out. Seeing their plight, Porter Williams went to a sleeper car, collected the hammocks used for beds, tied them together and helped all the passengers to escape the car. Then he led the terrified survivors across the wreckage of the train to safety. Helping passengers to disembark from the train was his job. It was that simple. He took it seriously. Minutes later the now empty car toppled into the raging creek. **Fight on!**

Repentant Hero

A captain named Burden was assigned a job in the War Department in Washington D.C. in the late Nineteenth Century. Things were going his way. His military career was moving steadily in the right direction and he was in love with a beautiful young lady. But the young lady met a private in the cavalry by the name of Hardey and switched affections, leaving Captain Burden greatly grieved. Since the Spanish-American War was on, the disheartened captain put in for a transfer to a front line cavalry company in Cuba, where the fighting was hot.

Upon arrival he was assigned a dangerous reconnaissance mission just before the attack on El Caney. His commanding officer supplied him with two volunteers, a Corporal Joyce and a Private Hardey. Yes, that Private Hardey. As they stole through the darkness, Captain Burden cunningly directed Pvt. Hardey to the left while he and Joyce would work around to the right. Going to the left would send Hardey directly into Spanish emplacements. It was kin to murder and Burden knew it. But the captain's conscience ate at the evil act he had committed. As he mused, shots rang out and the plaintive voice of Pvt. Hardey was heard above the sound of rifle and pistol shots.

At the sound, Captain Burden bolted toward the wounded trooper calling to him as he went, followed closely by Cpl. Joyce. They arrived to see Hardey laying on his side firing at five Spanish soldiers with his pistol. When the Americans appeared, the Spaniards, fearing an American attack, fell back. As he pulled his pistol, Burden turned to Joyce, and cried,

"Corporal, to the rear with Private Hardey; I'll cover you." Joyce threw the wounded soldier over his shoulder and headed back to camp. Behind them could be heard the Spanish Mauser rifles being answered by the repentant captain's revolver. Then there was only silence.

Private Hardey survived, married and lived out his life. Captain Burden's body was found the next day. He had done wrong but refused to stay wrong. **Do right!**

"I'm very careful what I do. I realize that what I say will be represented not only as a Viet Nam veteran, but as a Medal of Honor recipient, and the media will have a field day. If I get stopped drinking and driving, it's going to say 'Medal of Honor Winner Drunk.' I realize that. I'm not going to bring shame on either the medal or myself, so I do watch it very carefully."

(John L. Levitow, from a 1986 interview)

Twenty Seconds to Hell

THOUSANDS of Douglas DC-3's died in Air Corps duty during World War II as C-47's. But, almost thirty years later many were still flying. A number of those had been converted to AC-47 gun ships, call sign "Spooky." The AC-47 had three 7.62 mm mini guns which protruded from the windows on the left side of the aircraft. The aircraft commander would bank the plane into a slow left turn and the guns, firing 3,000 rounds per minute, could place one bullet in every square foot of a football field.

On the night of February 24, 1969, "Spooky 71" was directed to Long Biah where an Army base was under heavy attack. The plane made a gun pass, silencing the 82 mm mortars which had been hammering the base. A mile south another mortar battery opened up and aircraft commander, Maj. Kenneth B. Carpenter, banked toward the new target.

Since most enemy attacks took place at night, most Spooky missions did also. Prior to a gun pass, a crew member would throw three foot long, five inch round, magnesium flares out of the cargo door on the plane's left side. The flares, with two million candle power, would float down by parachute, providing light for the gun pass. Before jettisoning the flare, a safety pin was removed. Twenty seconds after its removal a small explosion would ignite the flare.

The crewman had his finger in the loop of the safety pin, ready to pull it and toss out the flare, when an 82 mm shell hit the airplane on the right wing. The resulting explosion blew a two foot hole in the wing, severed fuel lines and peppered the fuselage with 3,500 pieces of shrapnel. Forty of those pieces of shrapnel slammed into the body of A1C John L. Levitow. All the crew behind the flight deck was wounded. The explosion threw them all to the deck and caused the plane to drop into a right hand bank. In being tossed about, the flare had been ripped from the crewman's hand. All he held was the safety pin. In twenty seconds the flare would ignite and a 4,000 degree sun would melt its way into 19,000 lbs. of ammunition and then burn through the aircraft deck, severing control cables. The plane was doomed.

While helping a wounded crew member, Levitow spotted the flare which had rolled against an ammunition case. Unable to stand or even crawl, Levitow dragged himself over to the flare as valuable seconds ticked by. The wounded airman couldn't grasp the flare so he laid over top of it, held it to himself and continued what amounted to an uphill crawl toward the cargo door. His wounds left a trail of blood on the cabin floor. Levitow reached the door and with heroic determination heaved the flare overboard...at the exact second it ignited, but it was out of the airplane and caused no further damage.

Major Carpenter nursed the wounded bird home and all crewmen survived. A1C Levitow was awarded the medal of honor.

John L. Levitow died of cancer November 8, 2000, at age fifty-five. **Fight on!**

Pistolareo to the Rescue

IT was during the Apache Indian War of 1886 that the 4th Cavalry pursued a raiding Indian war party across the border into Mexico. On May 3 they engaged the Apaches in a vicious fight. In the heat of the fight, a young corporal got separated from the rest of his troop. He was wounded and fell from his horse and immediately set upon by the Indians. Only one trooper witnessed this action, Lieutenant Powhatan Clark. Lt. Clark knew he had to act fast, so, looking like a character in a John Wayne movie, he charged alone into the red horde with a pistol blazing in each hand. His one-man attack stunned the Indians, drove them off and secured the safety of the wounded trooper. **Fight on!**

The Price of Nice

ON February 23, 1991, a small Special Forces reconnaissance team was inserted near an Iraqi highway. No sooner had they landed than they set off dogs barking, probably belonging to local shepherds. With their position compromised and limited darkness left, they quickly headed for a pre-planned "hide point." They dug in just before dawn, but now their real troubles began.

With dawn came hordes of local Bedouin shepherds. It was just a short time before they were discovered by a Bedouin and his little daughter. They had two choices, kill them both to protect themselves or allow these two "Innocents" to live and put their own lives in danger.

The American fighting man is the fiercest warrior history has ever known, but, he is not a cold-blooded killer. They let them live. Due to these Americans' natural kindness, the alarm went out. The Bedouins, not appreciating the value of mercy and hoping to receive money from the Iraqi government for capturing the Americans, fired on them. The Special Forces troops headed for a drainage ditch while the Bedouins flagged down a large Iraqi convoy.

The Special Forces troops set up a defensive position and called for a hot extraction even while the Iraqi troops opened up on them. The battle for survival began in earnest as the Iraqis poured fire into the American position, while the Americans in return had to try to conserve ammunition. For two hours they desperately fought to keep the Iraqis from overrunning them. Finally, an F-16 flew in and attacked the enemy troops, killing almost fifty of them and hampering their attack. But there were a lot of Iraqis, and they were determined to kill these Americans.

Finally, a lone MH-60 Black Hawk helicopter, piloted by Chief Warrant Officer, James Chrisatulli, came screaming in at an altitude of 6 feet. As his door gunners provided covering fire, Chrisatulli dropped his bird right in the middle of the raging firefight to retrieve the beleaguered troopers. Chrisatulli sat there listening to Iraqi rounds slamming into his craft, yet he refused to take off until every Special Forces trooper was accounted for and aboard. Then amid a hail of bullets, he forced his wounded bird into the air and vacated the area. He and his co-pilot received the Distinguished Flying Cross, their aircraft was permanently out of the war and a handful of Special Forces troops would live to fight again. **Fight on!**

"I want to make public acknowledgment that I believe in God the Father Almighty. I want all you officers and men to lift up your hats, and from your hearts offer silent thanks to the Almighty."

Captain John W. Philip, captain of the battleship USS Texas, *after the Americans had defeated the Spanish fleet off Santiago, Cuba, July 3, 1898.*

Gallant Revenge!

DURING the Spanish-American War, Spain's mighty fleet lay hold up in the harbor of Santiago, Cuba. Outside the harbor, a fleet of American ships waited for them to come out and fight. Instead, early on Sunday morning, July 3, 1898, they sprinted from the harbor hoping to outrun their American pursuers. Their sleek, Spanish armored cruisers, firing as they went, sought to break into the open sea. Three American battleships, the *Texas*, the *Iowa,* the *Oregon* and armored cruiser, *Brooklyn,* gave chase and engaged the enemy ships. The Spanish ships had the advantage of being under the umbrella of fire from two Spanish forts high on the coast above them. To fire on the Spaniards, the American ships would have to enter the circle of death from above. Soon, through the smoke of battle, two of the Spanish ships could be seen beached and burning. But in smoke is confusion and in confusion is opportunity and the Spanish were prepared to exploit that opportunity.

While everyone's attention was focused on the eight capital ships, two fast Spanish destroyers burst from the mist on a torpedo attack. Their target was the American cruiser *Brooklyn*. She was theirs for the taking - but she would not be taken.

To lose a ship, for whatever reason, is a great shame to its captain and death to his naval career. Lieutenant-Commander Richard Wainwright had been the executive officer of the battleship *Maine* when it was blown up and sunk in the Havana harbor. Wainwright's next command was the lowly *Gloucester*, nothing more than a converted yacht with four meager six-pounder guns. That Sunday morning the *Gloucester* was all that stood between the Spanish attack and the doomed *Brooklyn*. Never mind that it was two-to-one. Never mind that he was outgunned, his puny six-pounders against 12 and 14 pounders aboard the destroyers. Never mind that, to cut off the attackers, he also had to sail into the ring of destruction from both forts on the cliffs above. These were the ones who had sunk his ship!

The water boiled behind the *Glouscester* as she turned into the onrushing Spaniards. Fire belched from his tiny six-pounders and, while his antagonist's shots missed, his found their mark. That stopped the attack and saved the *Brooklyn*. Soon the other Americans joined in and the two destroyers were sent to the bottom. Ironically, it was Captain Wainwright's ship that was to capture Spanish Admiral Cervera, the commander of the Spanish fleet. And Lieutenant-Commander Wainwright had exacted his revenge. **Fight on!**

The Best Defense

HAVING won the Battle of Bladensburg and burned the "President's House" (soon to be white-washed and become famous as the "White House"), the British sailed for New Orleans. Victory there would shut down the port and open the interior of the United States to attack via the Mississippi River.

General Andrew Jackson arrived in New Orleans December 1, 1814. Rather than sit behind breastworks and await the enemy, his plan was to assault them the moment they landed.

At 1PM on December 23, word reached Jackson that the British had landed 15 miles below New Orleans. That very evening his army pounced on the British with the fury of a mother bear. In less than a half-an-hour 700 Red Coats were killed, 1,400 wounded and 500 captured at the expense of seven wounded Americans. Then Jackson's small force fell back to their defense and prepared for the attack.

On January 8, 1815, it came. Waves of British regulars assaulted Jackson's cotton- bale breastworks but fell before the determined American gunfire. In twenty-five minutes the British lost 2,600 men killed and wounded - and the battle. Jackson suffered eight killed and thirteen wounded. **Fight on!**

> Children's children are
> the crown of old men;
> and the glory of children
> are their fathers.
>
> *Proverbs 17:6*

A Father to Be Proud Of

DOCTOR James Reddick, a Seattle dentist, and his son, 11 year old David, and his daughter, 12 year old Sharon, decided to hike the trail that would take them 4,500 feet up the side of Mt. Rainier to Camp Muir on Friday, June 1, 1968.

Suddenly a storm blew in. Winds up to 60 mph lashed at the carefree trio as the temperature plummeted to 22 degrees. There was a wind chill of -30 degrees as the snowfield was veiled in a whiteout of fog and blowing snow.

The three desperately dug a shallow trench, roofed it with a tarp anchored by their backpacks and climbed in. Reddick placed his wet, shivering children in a sleeping bag and wrapped one around himself. But there was a problem. The opening they crawled through poured sub-zero air into the coffin-like enclosure. The children were freezing. At that point the 51 year old father backed himself against the opening, sealing it off, but exposing his back to the brutal temperatures. Before long the children noticed that their father wasn't talking as much as he had, although he assured them that they would be rescued.

The storm blew all day Saturday not breaking until early Sunday morning. Rescuers fanned out on the mountain and came upon the snow covered packs. David and Sharon lived but for that to happen it cost their father his life. **Thank you, Dad.**

Don't Mess With Me

(*Author's Note:* The men of the Old West were definitely hard cases. They had to be to survive in such a harsh, savage land. We, addicted to air conditioning and fast food, shouldn't be too quick to judge them.)

SMOKEY Thompson was a buffalo hunter in north Texas in the late 1800s. He carried a single shot muzzle loader. Thompson was an old salt who was as tough as they came. He simply wanted to do his business and be left alone. It wasn't to be. One day Thompson was out on the plains on foot when he heard the cries of an Indian war party. Since Thompson wasn't a guilt-ladened college graduate of the Twentieth Century he was unaware that torturing white men was just an innocent part of the Indian's "proud heritage." So, as the Indians attacked, he simply raised his rifle and fired. The Indians veered off. Lacking rifles, they shot arrows at Thompson as he casually walked in the direction of his camp. If they got too close he'd turn and raise his rifle and the braves would retreat. Finally, the Indian leader decided to press the issue and rode straight for the hunter. Not the thing to do. Thompson raised his rifle and fired, killing the man. Knowing he had no time to reload, the remaining Indians charged, certain of victory. The quick, and quick-thinking Thompson dashed for the fallen Indian's horse, catching the rope hanging from its neck. With six screaming Indians barreling down on him Thompson needed to mount up and escape. But he didn't. Before mounting the Indian's pony, he defiantly pulled his knife, cut a circle around the top of the Indian's head and with a "pop" yanked off his his scalp. Then he mounted his new horse and rode off. **Fight on!**

Get It!

ALEXANDER Graham Bell was a "Professor of Speech Physiology" at the School of Oratory of Boston University. In 1875 Bell took a crude electrical device to Dr. Joseph Henry, the first Secretary of the Smithsonian Institute. Rather than sending the 28 year old away with his foolish ideas, the 80 year old doctor listened to Bell's thoughts, inspected his machine and said, "You have the germ of a great invention, work at it."

But Alexander Graham Bell, who had been ridiculed, mocked and nearly disheartened by the cruel puns of his friends, explained that he wasn't qualified to pursue the task any farther. He explained that, as a speech therapist, he did not possess the knowledge of electricity needed to figure out how to send the human voice via an electrical current. Rather than agree or sympathize, Henry fixed his gaze on the young inventor and simply said, "Get it."

Those two words heartened the discouraged young inventor's soul. They drove him to learn what he needed to know about electricity. They kept him going through numerous failures and criticism. Ultimately, they spurred him on to success.

What is it that you lack that's keeping you from success? **Get it!**

An Officer and A Warrior

(*Author's Note:* People who know nothing about the military love to pontificate on the fact that American officers "lead from the rear." Actually, up to the rank of full bird colonel, U.S. officers lead their men into combat - from the front. Above that rank, general officers are no longer able to lead men into battle because the number of troops they command is simply too great for one individual to lead.)

LIEUTENANT Colonel John Page, U.S. Army, knew only one thing: Kill the enemy. During the fighting retreat of American forces from the Choshin Reservoir in Korea in late 1950, the colonel never let a chance to kill Communist Chinese troops pass. Nearing a damaged bridge, enemy forces pinned down the American column. Colonel Page crawled out and killed the enemy troops.

At Koto-ri he assembled stray Army soldiers into a reserve force to back up the Marines fighting there. Then he helped construct an airstrip in the besieged village. Twice when Chinese Communist forces threatened the strip, Page led American forces to secure it. Once secure, he flew off with a pilot. To safety? No. Although he could have flown to safety, he instead had the pilot buzz enemy foxholes while he dropped hand grenades and sprayed them with rifle fire.

Next he flew to a near area and arranged artillery support for the retreating Americans and then flew back to rejoin the retreat. When the column neared Funchilin Pass it was attacked from both sides of the road. Lt. Col. Page mounted a damaged tank and fired away at the enemy, thus allowing the American vehicles to pass. In the middle of the pass, Chinese soldiers fired down on the Americans from the steep hillside above. Lt. Col.

Page got a machine gun, climbed the hill and pinned down the enemy while the Americans continued south.

On December 10, as they tried to emerge from the pass, the Chinese stopped them with a strong force to their front and both flanks. The battle raged the entire length of the column. Lt. Col. Page fought his way to the front of the column and then plunged into the enemy in a one man attack. His action disoriented the enemy who fell back. Page followed through, at times going hand-to-hand with the enemy. The Chinese broke and ran. The Americans escaped the trap. Lieutenant Colonel John U. D. Page, an officer and a warrior, had fought his last battle on the frozen ground of Funchilin Pass. He was posthumously awarded the Medal of Honor. **Fight on!**

O God, thou hast taught me from my youth: and hitherto have I declared thy wondrous works.

Now also when I am old and greyheaded, O God, forsake me not; until I have shewed thy strength unto *this* generation, *and* thy power to every one *that* is to come.

Psalm 71:17, 18

Never Too Old

LEVI Smith was a lumberjack in Washington State until he was 63 years old. He also pastored a little church. Then, at 63, the determined old Christian went to Japan as a missionary! He was there for 33 years! At 96 he came home. But after spending one year back in the United States he said, "God's not through with me yet in Japan." At age 97 he returned to Japan. He died there at age 98! We all should be so tough. **Fight on!**

Hero Without a Gun

ON April 25, 1915, at the height of World War I a contingent from the Australian and New Zealand armies were landed at what was to become known as "ANZAC Cove" at Gallipoli in the Mediterranean Sea. But the bowl-shaped cove was not the correct landing area and the defenseless troopers lay in the open, surrounded by hills where over 45,000 Turkish troops could fire down on them. Soon, wounded "Diggers" were everywhere with no way to be evacuated back to the beach. As men hunkered down to escape the incessant sniper fire a strange being appeared out of the smoke of the battle. That "being" was John Simpson Kirkpatrick, a private in the Australian Medical Corps leading a donkey. Twenty-two year old Kirkpatrick had no way to carry wounded men back down to the beach so he rounded up a stray donkey and, oblivious to death whizzing around him, carried man after man back to safety. Men buried in foxholes would call to the private warnings of the danger he was in, but he would cheerfully wave and answer back, "my troubles."

For twenty-four days Kirkpatrick made his selfless trips bringing back as many as a dozen men a day. In the hills above, Turkish snipers made an effort to hit him as he walked haplessly through the fire. Orders were given for all ambulance workers not to venture out because of the ferocity of the battle. But the "bloke and his donk" never stopped delivering wounded men to the aid station.

On May 19, 1915, as Kirkpatrick was rescuing yet another Digger, he was hit in the back by a Turkish machine gun. He died instantly.

Today, outside the Australian War Memorial in Canberra, Australia, there stands a bronze statue of Kirkpatrick and his donkey carrying a wounded soldier to safety. In 1965, five different Australian postage stamps were issued with Kirkpatrick's likeness on the them. In 1967, the Australian government struck the ANZAC Commemorative Medallion to honor those who endured Gallipoli. It bears the image of the Canberra statue. In 1995, Australia issued a five dollar commemorative gold coin with the same image on it. The man, his donkey and a wounded comrade are also immortalized on the Australian one hundred dollar bill. **Fight on!**

Grant's Victory for the South

THE detractors of General Ulysses S. Grant love to deride him as "just a drunk." He was. Yet the general restricted his drinking to those times away from his family. At home, and later as president, he was always decidedly sober.

Furthermore, credit is seldom given him for his grace in victory. When others sought to humiliate and completely crush the South, Grant, like Lincoln, preached restraint and reconciliation. His gracious stipulation allowing Confederate officers to keep their horses, swords and sidearms greatly relieved Gen. Robert E. Lee and his men. Then he went further and stipulated that the cavalry and men in the artillery could also retain their horses so they could plow their fields back home. To this, a grateful Gen. Lee responded, "This will have a very happy effect upon my army."

But others were not so gracious and, unbeknownst to Gen. Grant, he had one more battle to fight in the Civil War: A battle for the South

Shortly after the war ended, while Gen. Grant was in Washington, he received some very disturbing news. Secretary of War Stanton had, in disregard of the terms of surrender, issued an order for the arrest of Robert E. Lee and numerous other Southern leaders. Gen. Grant hurried to the Secretary's office and boldly confronted him, "Mr. Secretary, when General Lee surrendered to me at Appomattox, I gave him my word of honor that neither he nor any of his followers would be disturbed so long as they obeyed their parole of honor. I have learned nothing to cause me to believe that any of my late adversaries have broken their promises, and I have come here to make you aware of that fact, and to suggest that your orders be canceled."

Incredulous at Grant's willful insubordination, Secretary Stanton reminded him sternly, "General Grant, are you aware of whom you are talking to? I am the Secretary of War."

Without an ounce of intimidation in his response, the fearless Union general instantly fired back, "And I am General Grant. Issue those orders at your peril."

Whether a bluff or a promise we will never know. Suddenly Secretary Stanton no longer felt inclined to arrest any of the South's leaders. A great national rift was prevented and the very last battle of the Civil War was fought. It was a Northern victory.....for the South. **Remember.**

A Tea Kettle, a Pistol and a Good Man

ON December 12, 1811, the brig, *Polly*, left Boston harbor bound for the West Indies with a cargo of lumber. Three days out she encountered a vicious gale. During the storm a huge wave swept over her, laid her on her side and filled her with water. The men that crewed the ship chopped the masts off, righting the waterlogged hulk, but not before they had lost their two sole passengers.

Captain Andrew Cazneau and his six crewmen now drifted helplessly as the gale drove them out to sea, kept afloat by the ship's load of lumber. Men dove into the water-filled hold and secured a little meat and fresh water stored below. They also retrieved a tea kettle and a flint lock pistol.

When the storm finally died the ship was left adrift in the Gulf Stream, slowly headed for Africa. They were sure they would be sighted by another ship and rescued but no ships hove into view.

Days became weeks and finally they exhausted their meat supply. The mate, a Mr. Pollack, was the first to die. It had been fifty days since the gale had destroyed their ship. Seaman Howe followed him six days later.

The next day the men caught and killed a patrolling shark. With meat secured, their most pressing need was for fresh water. Their water supply was exhausted. Captain Cazneau pondered the iron teakettle and flint lock pistol his men had secured from below. The men had spoken of throwing the worthless items overboard but the captain wondered how he could use them to save his men's lives. It struck him! He turned, placed the tea kettle upside down on top of their cooking pot and sealed the seam with strips of cloth. Then he disassembled the pistol and jammed the barrel up into the inverted spout. He filled his invention with sea water and placed it on the fire they kept going in the galley stove. As the water boiled men poured cold water on the outside of the teakettle causing the steam within to condense and run out the gun barrel as water. The captain had manufactured a crude fresh water still! Soon they were producing five precious pints a day.

Shortly their shark meat was exhausted and the captain thought of another food source. He had his men dive and scrape the barnacles off the hull and they ate them raw. This lasted them another thirty-eight days before the hull was picked clean. Again the men grew physically faint. Ninety-one days after the storm, the cook died. The men were desperate for food so they cut off the dead man's legs. To eat? No! To use as shark bait. Soon they were feasting on another freshly caught shark.

Weeks went by and another sailor died, leaving Captain Cazneau and two remaining seamen on board the hulk as it drifted into the Sargasso Sea, that portion of the Atlantic that is crammed with drifting seaweed. But this was not a bad thing, for the wise captain hauled up huge amounts of seaweed and picked out the small crabs and tiny fish that resided there. Again his resourcefulness spread a welcome table for his dwindling crew. Days went by and they continued drifting, leaving the Sargasso Sea behind.

May came. Five months adrift and another seaman gave up the fight. Finally, one morning they sighted the sail of a distant ship. Hope revived...until it sailed from view having missed seeing the low-riding, mastless *Polly*. But now they knew they were nearing the shipping lanes. Almost daily they sighted the sails of passing ships. But every time the ships proceeded on their courses unaware of the floating refugees.

Captain Cazneau encouraged his remaining crewman, Seaman Badger, to hang on. They simply had to be sighted by one passing ship soon. May came and went. Then June. On the 20th of June, 1812, the men's prayers were answered as no fewer than three ships headed for the wreck. The English ship, *Fame*, took them on board and tended to them. One hundred and ninety-one days had passed since the wreck.

On July 9, they were put on board an American ship headed for Maine. A few days later the family of the amazing captain was astounded as the long lost seaman strode into his home. **Fight on!**

A Private Fight

THE time was November, 1938. The place was Shanghai, China. To this day no one knows what started it, but two Marines were hammering away at each other right out in public. Strangely, when one man could take no more and went down, the other would stop fighting and help him up...then they'd go back to fighting - repeating the process over and over. Before long a group of sailors came by, watched for a while, and decided it was time for the fight to end. It was a mistake. The two Jarheads turned on the would-be peacemakers, and soon sailors were down on the ground all around them. That little issue taken care of, the two persistent Marines turned their attention back to each other. They had definitely decided to....**Fight On!**

"The first half I ran as fast as I could. The second half I ran faster with God's help."

Eric Liddell, after recovering from a fall and winning a race.

The Runner With Heart

ERIC Liddell was born in China to his parents, James and Mary, in 1902. They had left their native Scotland to go to China as missionaries. When Eric was only six, he and his brother Robert, eight, were placed in The School for the Sons of Missionaries in London. He stood out in track and field events and, after entering Edinburgh University, developed into the fastest man in Scotland. He set many best records, some of which still haven't been broken.

In February of 1923, the best athletes of England, Scotland and Ireland met to see who would represent Great Britain in the 1924 Olympic Games in Paris. Although the 100 and 200 yard races were his strong suit, Liddell also entered the 440. The starter's pistol sounded and they were off. But suddenly a competitor tripped and stumbled into Liddell, slamming him into the turf. Dazed and confused, Liddell turned to see the officials motioning him to resume running against a field of runners that was 60 feet ahead of him. The young Christian launched himself in pursuit. By the time the runners reached the home stretch, Liddell was 4th and chasing the leader who was still 30 feet ahead of him. With a super human effort he moved to third, then second and finally first, winning the event by 6 feet.
Fight On!

(*Author's Note:* Eric Liddell was immortalized in the film, *Chariots of Fire*, which records his refusal to run the 100 meters, his best event, in the 1924 Olympics because it was held on Sunday. He instead entered the 200 and 400 meters, placing 3rd in the 200 and winning the gold in the 400, setting a new world record of 42.6 seconds. But then he truly showed his champion character. He left Scotland to return to China as a missionary like his parents. He died there in January of 1945 in a Japanese internment camp.)

You Do What You Gotta Do

CHARLES P. Bartley, operator of Alaska Adventure, an air taxi service at Snowshoe Lake in Alaska, had just deposited two hunters at their cabin on Tazlina Lake. By the time he was ready to take off, the wind had picked up and he knew the three foot waves would be a task for his Cessna 180 float plane to overcome.

After an aborted attempt, Bartley taxied out around a spit of land looking for calmer water not knowing his earlier attempt had damaged a float which was rapidly filling with water. The float settled and a gust of wind caught the opposite uplifted wing, flipping the plane over. Bartley escaped, climbing onto the watertight float. He was out of sight of the cabin he'd just left.

Dennis Pollard, friend and fellow pilot, had left the lake just ahead of Bartley. Arriving back at Snowshoe Lake, Pollard was alarmed when Bartley never returned. He returned to Tazlina and questioned the hunters who had no idea what had become of him. Pollard took off.

Hours later, now with a spotter, Pollard returned to Tazina and spotted Bartley's chilled form straddling his airplane pontoon. Dropping his light Super Cub onto the choppy waters, they taxied over to him but wind and waves prevented them from taking the hypothermic man on board. Failing at that, Pollard took off again, climbed to 5,000 feet so his radio transmission would clear the mountains and called Search and Rescue. Numerous bush pilots scrambled when they heard the call as an HH60 helicopter was also launched.

Seventy-one year old Al Lee piloted his Beaver for the

lake. But the waves were fully four feet and too much to set down on. As Lee pondered, a Bell 206 Jet Ranger helicopter arrived. Lee circled and watched as the pilot hovered at the wreckage. As his assistant tried to pull the nearly helpless Bartley from the water, the copter tilted low on one side. Just then a wave reached up striking the rotor and pulled the helicopter into the lake where it rapidly sank. Now there were three men adrift. Bartley had been hit by the helicopter's skid as it flipped and was now seriously injured. Five thousand feet above, Al Lee knew the men were in big trouble and the HH60 was still 30 minutes away. Casting away his earlier caution, Lee headed for the lake's foaming surface. The Beaver bounced and shuddered as it hit the surface. Surprised he was still alive and afloat, Lee taxied over and was able to get the three on board. But there was no way he would ever get airborne again with all aboard. He taxied three miles to a cove. Twenty minutes later the HH60 landed and took his charges.

    The floats on Lee's plane had been damaged by shoreline rocks where Bartley had been off-loaded. Lee pumped them empty of lake water and then made a hasty takeoff. He explained his dynamic landing on the violent water with, "You do what you gotta do." **Fight on!**

A Brief Stop for Guidance

TO those who work with him at his office at Deloittes Touche in Wilton, Ct., David Karnes is an accountant. But to his fellow Marines, he was Staff Sergeant Karnes who had spent 23 years in active and reserve Marines units until 1998.

On the morning of September 11, 2001, Karnes sister called him to tell him about the attack on the World Trade Center. Over forty miles distance meant nothing to Karnes. He hopped into his Porsche and veritably flew to Long Island. There he picked up his Marine gear. But before heading for the disaster he made one more stop. He headed to his church, Bible Baptist Church in Elmont, NY, and asked the pastor, Rev. James Barker, to ask the Lord to lead him to a survivor. Then he headed into the heart of the disaster.

While Karnes was heading south, events in New York City were deteriorating. The towers of the Trade Center collapsed. Then at 5:30 PM building Number 7 also fell. Rescuers had pulled back a bit.

SSgt. Karnes spied another Marine and announced, "Hey, devil dog, we need you in there."

"Aye, aye, staff sergeant," came the reply without hesitation. Then together they headed into the smoke. Making their way atop the treacherous wreckage, they would call out, "U.S. Marines, if you can hear us, yell or clap." After several hours Karnes spied a hole in the rubble and headed for it.

Thirty feet beneath the wreckage, Port Authority police officers, Will Jimeno and Sgt. John McLoughlin, were injured and trapped. For hours they had called for help. Then, through the darkness, Jimeno heard, "U.S. Marines, if you can hear us, yell or clap."

"10-13! 10-13! McLoughlin and Jimeno, Port Authority Police Department. We're here! We're here! Please don't leave us."

Thirty feet above him, a man much bigger than his physical size called down, "I'm not leaving you buddy. You're coming out!" SSgt. Karnes climbed right down into the hole with the trapped men and stayed there till they were rescued. It took hours to free the two police officers, but both survived. And Staff Sergeant Karnes? He re-enlisted in the active Marine reserves and put in for a posting on the front line in the Middle East! **Fight on!**

Who can find a virtuous woman? for her price *is* far above rubies.

The heart of her husband doth safely trust in her, so that he shall have no need of spoil.

She will do him good and not evil all the days of her life.

Proverbs 31:10 - 12

A Virtuous Woman

CAPTAIN Harry Hunt, captain of a coastal transport, was married to the beautiful Janie Scadden in the summer of 1863. Then the wedding party all boarded his boat in New York harbor for a celebratory cruise. They had hardly left port when Hunt's vessel was hailed and halted by Union authorities. Hunt and his ship were needed immediately to haul a shipment of corn from North Carolina to New York. Wedding party and all, the vessel set its course for southern coastal waters.

While the ship was being loaded, Confederate troops stormed in and captured the ship, its cargo and all aboard. Seeing that the wedding party were noncombatants, Southern officers released all on board, including the new Mrs. Hunt. Only her husband would be taken prisoner. But young Janie had not married Harry just to lose him, and she refused to leave him. Unbelievably, both were eventually sent to the infamous Andersonville Prison where the ground was all mud and goo and human filth lay everywhere. Over 12,000 men would die from the inhumane conditions.

Captain and Mrs. Hunt and a chest of their belongings, including $5,000 in cash, took up housekeeping in a meager tent within the gruesome prison. But some people in prison belong in prison and one night the back of their tent was slit and their chest and its contents were spirited away.

Now, this incredible woman, alone among an ocean of destitute and desperate men, had to make due with what little that remained.

Thirteen months after their capture, Mrs. Hunt gave birth to a baby boy amidst the squalor that was Andersonville.

One day, a passing Confederate doctor was surprised to hear the cry of a baby in the midst of such an awful place. He stopped and talked with Mrs. Hunt and heard her story. Greatly moved by the resolute character of this stately lady, he managed to have her and her baby removed from the prison and boarded at a nearby farm. He then procured material so the mother and child could have clean, decent clothes. Next, he arranged to have Captain Hunt paroled to work in the prison hospital so he could be with his wife.

The unbending courage and resolve of this brave lady resulted in hardship for herself, but ultimately wrought freedom for her and her whole family. **Virtue!**

Circular Reasoning

A PBY Catalina is a large, twin-engined, flying boat used for rescue and reconnaissance during World War II. It is not built to do combat with enemy fighters and was no match for one agile Japanese Zero, let alone four. But that's how many Zeroes attacked a PBY piloted by Lt. C. E. Rodebaugh in December of 1943 while flying near the Aleutian islands. The low, slow twin-engine patrol craft didn't stand a chance against the agile fighters. But Lt. Rodebaugh's quick thinking saved them as he threw his plane into a tight circle around the volcanic cone of Segula Island and just held the airplane in a tight circle around the cone. Every time a Japanese fighter tried to maneuver behind the lumbering aircraft Rodebaugh's turret gunners hammered away at it. While the confused enemy pilots pondered how to get at the big plane Rodebaugh saw his chance and dove into a small bay and then climbed into the clouds where he lost his attackers. Then he lumbered on back to his base. **Fight on!**

Some trust in chariots, and some in horses: but we will remember the name of the LORD our God.

They are brought down and fallen: but we are risen, and stand upright.

Save, LORD: let the king hear us when we call.

Psalm 20:7 - 9

Singin' in the Rain

THE hurricane that hit Galveston September 8, 1900, had winds of 130 mph. The highest point on the island city of almost 38,000 people is only ten feet above hightide. The storm surge sent waves cascading through the city. Houses and buildings were systematically blown down by the winds or pounded down by the raging surf. Six thousand and three hundred people died that day.

At the Union Depot, passengers rushed upstairs as water surged in. They huddled in an upstairs room as waves battered the building's foundation. The wind began tearing off pieces of the roof. Around them building after building tumbled down. With death so close and help so far they did a strange thing. Rather than panic or despair they turned to the only source of hope. They all joined their voices in a hymn written by Charles Wesley, "Jesus Lover of My Soul."

Jesus, Lover of my soul, Let me to Thy bosom fly,
While the nearer waters roll, While the tempest still is high!
Hide me, O my Saviour, hide, Till the storm of life is past;
Safe into the haven guide, O receive my soul at last!

There was no "moment of silence," no pleas to false gods, no representative of the oppressive ACLU to bully them into silence because the hymn was not politically correct. Just a forlorn group of desperate creatures turning to their Creator at their hour of need. He heard them. The building held. They survived. They had turned events over to One who could do more than they could. **Pray!**

"Before God, I believe the hour has come. My judgement approves this measure, and my whole heart is in it. All that I have, and all that I am, and all that I hope in this life, I am now ready here to stake upon it. And I leave off as I began, that live or die, survive or perish, I am for the Declaration. It is my living sentiment, and by the blessing of God it shall be my dying sentiment, Independence Now, and Independence forever!"

(John Adams urging the Continental Congress to approve the Declaration of Independence)

God give us Men!
A time like this demands
Strong minds, great hearts,
True faith and ready hands;
Men whom the lust of office does not kill;
Men whom the spoils of office cannot buy;
Men who possess opinions and a will;
Men who have honor - men who will not lie;
Tall men, sun-crowned,
Who live above the fog
In public duty and in private thinking.
(At the dedication of Samuel Adams memorial in his church.)

"It is the duty of all nations to acknowledge the providence of the Almighty God, to obey his will, to be grateful for his benefits, and humbly to implore his protection and favor."

"I have called on Thee for pardon and forgiveness of sins...accept and answer for the sake of Thy Dear Son, Jesus Christ our Lord, Amen."

George Washington

More Than a Bridge

BETWEEN Trenton and Princeton, New Jersey, lies a bridge over Stony Brook Creek. It was imperative that it be destroyed to thwart a British advance. On January 3, 1777, the British 17th Regiment of Foot under Lt. Colonel Charles Mawhood fixed bayonets and charged Colonials holding the hill overlooking the strategic bridge. Bodies dropped beneath cold British steel as the Colonials began to drop back. Then the Colonial commander, Brigadier General Hugh Mercer, ran for the front crying, "No! Forward!" A British bayonet was driven into him, then another. British soldiers stabbed him more than a dozen times, then left his lifeless form to concentrate their attention on the faltering Americans. They slammed into another line of Colonials and again the field was littered with American bodies. Just as the battle was about to be lost, General George Washington spurred his horse to the front to rally his hesitant troops, stopping less than 100 feet from the onrushing British. It was the chance they had been waiting for. Redcoats raised their muskets and fired a volley at their enemy's commanding officer. A cloud of gunsmoke blotted out Washington and his troops for a few moments. But when it cleared, there sat Washington astride his horse still commanding his men. "Charge! Pull up! Pull up!" came his steel-like voice across the bloody battlefield. The inspired Colonials attacked and drove the British off the hill, destroyed the bridge and escaped.

It was only after this victory in the Battle of Princeton that the demand for American independence began to be taken seriously by the British and the rest of the world. After this battle the French began to send military supplies to the United States. General Washington's army was infused with new morale and enlistments finally began to increase. The victory won that day was far more than a little stone bridge, it was freedom. **Fight on!**

"We have no King but Jesus"
The rallying cry during the War for Independence

One Man vs. A Battalion

ON January 22, 1944, U.S. Army soldiers landed at Anzio beach on Italy's boot and moved inland. On February 1, the 1st Battalion, 30th Infantry Regiment was making good progress when it was attacked by a German battalion backed by artillery and tanks. The savageness of the attack resulted in the death or capture of the battalion's officers and most of the noncoms, leading the dazed survivors to pull back, with the Germans in hot pursuit.

Suddenly, German troopers began to drop due to the accurate fire of Private Alton Knappenberger and his Browning Automatic Rifle (BAR). To fire effectively, Pvt. Knappenberger had to situate himself on a small hill in plain sight of the Germans. It didn't take long for them to pay special attention to the 19 year old Pennsylvanian. A German platoon, armed with machine pistols, charged him but he dropped them all. Next, the enemy unleashed a machine gun on him. Knappenberger rose to one knee as German machine bullets kicked up dirt around him, aimed carefully and wiped out this new threat. But while he was occupied with the machine gun, two other Germans got close enough to hurl grenades at him. Dirt covered, helmet dented, ears ringing, the stalwart infantryman rose from the smoke as a second machine gun took him under fire. Calmly, Knappenberger hammered this new threat into oblivion. Suddenly the earth around the determined American began exploding as the Germans turned a 20 mm flak gun his direction. But that wasn't his greatest threat. A quick inventory told Knappenberger that he had shot up all 13 magazines for his

BAR. He turned and crawled to where another BAR man had fallen and crawled back with his ammo pouch. Again the unflappable private took careful aim and picked off the crew of the flak gun. This stubborn American had upset the German's timetable. Something had to be done. Another platoon charged up the hill to silence him but were silenced themselves by his persistent shooting.

For two hours the unmovable private held back the German advance. Then, seeing he was about to be overrun, he quietly pulled back to the remnant of his company. He was one of the twenty-four men left of the original 240.

While Knappenberger fought on, the American line was stabilized and prevented a breakthrough.

When it was suggested he receive a promotion, the unassuming Pennsylvanian refused, saying, "Nope, not me. They make you a corporal or sergeant, and then you have to work." (!)

Private Knappenberger was awarded the Medal of Honor.
Fight on!

Faithful Abraham

BY the mid-Nineteenth Century, Ile Derniere, an island off the southern coast of Louisiana, was a playground for the rich. A hurricane, striking it in early August 1856, over a month before the recognized hurricane season, turned it into a graveyard for these same people.

Over 300 revelers were enjoying "The Good Life" of Ile Derniere on Sunday, August 10, 1856. Lounging in the cottages, they contemplated the coming evening's Grand Ball at the Trade Winds Hotel. They became puzzled when the sea suddenly began to churn and flail while no wind or even a cloud was evident. Finally the wind came. But it came from the northwest rather than the Gulf. None of it made any sense. Soon driving rain and howling winds raked the island.

Captain Abraham Smith had heard the reports that a great hurricane was headed for the coast. With the sea frothing and other boats wisely electing to stay in St. Mary's harbor, Capt. Smith cast off all lines and headed for Ile Derniere to assist any of the residents who might need help during the blow. His island steamer, *Star*, bobbed like a cork as waves washed over it. Finally, the storm-battered craft dropped both anchors in the island's small harbor. The captain, who had to be tied to the helm during the turbulent journey, dropped both anchors and waited.

With the storm battering the defenseless cottages, the islanders sought the safety of the sturdily built Trade Winds and lost themselves in revelry.

In the bay the *Star's* anchors dragged until the cables snapped, sending the helpless ship toward the shore. The crew secured two new lines and then received a startling order from Captain Smith. "Cut away the upper works." The ship was heeling over so pronounced it was in danger of capsizing. With axes flying, the men chopped away the pilot house, cabins and even the smoke stacks. With less wind resistance, the anchors held. Then the Captain resumed his waiting. From within the hotel, the Captain heard waltz music. "Waltzing, are they? God help them, and God help everyone of us if that wind whips around to the south! Waltzing? Why the very wind is waltzing tonight with the hurricane as a partner!"

As the party goers danced, the wind did just what the captain feared it would do. The storm hit in earnest. While the people danced they could not know that one-by-one every other building on the island was being systematically destroyed. Suddenly dancers found their feet wet as the sea had risen to cover the fifteen foot tall island and undercut the building. Waves exploded through the door and windows and people screamed as now it was the building that was doing the dancing. Ceilings fell, stairways collapsed.

Outside, a huge wave lifted the *Star*, swept it to the highest sand dune on the island and drove it keel first into the sand. The brave ship would never sail again. But she and her brave captain still had work to do this night.

In the Trade Winds, the water was waist deep. The last candle flickered out, the walls buckled and finally the old building which had weathered many an earlier hurricane was swept away.

On the *Star*, Captain Abraham had waited long enough. With a line tied around him, he leaped into the boiling waters and frantically plucked anyone who floated within his reach. Although the island was under water, the depth on top of his dune was only four feet so he waded out time and again, snatching victims and returning and handing them to his crewmen. While the captain was on one of his journeys out of sight in the blackness, the crew suddenly felt his rope go slack. Urgently they hauled in the line and retrieved the limp form of the captain, still clutching an unconscious young girl. Both were pulled aboard. Both were alive! Both recovered.

That night the devastation of Ile Derniere was so complete that not even the foundation of one building remained. The island was wiped clean, save for the battered hulk that had been the *Star*, with her captain, her crew and her load of survivors. That night over 300 people perished. Fewer than fifty survived. Of that figure, thirty-six were on board the *Star* due to her brave captain's faithfulness. **Fight on!**

Lost His Glasses But Not His Head

TWENTY-FIVE year old William Jacobs got separated from his fellow skiers in Yosemite National Park's Badger Pass, February 3, 1946, when he lost his glasses. The near-sighted skier was trying to find his way back to the Ski Lodge when he was overtaken by a blizzard. Now, with zero visibility added to his natural handicap, the man was thoroughly lost. He was battered by the storm, the first of two he would endure, which lasted several days, dropped 32 inches of fresh snow and plunged temperatures to five degrees.

The hopeless skier stumbled onto a Park Service emergency cache of blankets and a toboggan. No cabin. No food. Just the cache. Rather than give in to hopelessness and despair, Jacobs used what he had. He used the toboggan to build a windbreak and then hunkered down and awaited rescue.

Eleven long, cold days later, after his parents had given him up for dead and returned home, two Park Rangers happened upon the makeshift shelter. In spite of his ordeal and two frozen toes, the intrepid skier walked out, led by his rescuers. **Fight on!**

Lethal Grudge

ALTHOUGH Ben Moore was a hunter he wasn't interested in hunting bear that crisp autumn day. He and his hunting partner were after moose. Moore had left his partner in their Jeep and walked down to a small clearing to look for prospects with his field glasses. He saw no moose, but a grizzly bear unexpectedly filled his view through the lens. Moore froze, knowing that movement can invite attack. Suddenly the animal exploded from the bush in a full charge. Moore grabbed the Ruger .357 on his hip, cocked it and just had time to fire as the bear reached him. Though the bullet buried itself in the animal's chest, it didn't faze it and the bear grabbed Moore by the leg with its teeth and pitched him through the air over his head. Moore no sooner hit the ground than the grizzly was on him again. It sank its teeth into his leg and shook him as Ben let fly with another shot that missed the animal. Then he pointed the pistol at the grizzly's belly and slammed a shot home that split the beast open. The animal turned and grabbed Moore by the head and bit down. Moore heard his skull cracking in the beast's jaws as his left eye popped out of the socket. But this bear had grabbed hold of the wrong man! Moore was lying on his back with the bear standing over him. He was not going to play dead and he was not going to lay there too paralyzed with fear to fight back. Again he brought the pistol up, but the bear, seeing the movement, clamped down on both of Moore's hands. The man's hands, still holding the Ruger, were completely in the grizzly's mouth when he pulled the trigger. That got a reaction. The bear shook his head, swatted half-heartedly at the gun and turned and stumbled off. With blood pouring from his head wounds and his left eye hanging down on his cheek, Ben managed to get three new shells into his pistol, force himself to his feet and bellowed a challenge to the bear to come back and finish the issue. The bear declined.

Minutes later, Moore's hunting partner, having heard the shots, came upon him. He helped Moore back to the Jeep and he was eventually taken to Fairbanks Memorial Hospital.

It took plastic surgeons six operations to put Ben Moore back together, but he's not the same. Oh, it's not his face. It's his attitude. Now when he goes hunting, it's not for moose. It's for bear. **Fight back!**

The Angel of Marye's Heights

THE Union Army was defeated, no, massacred, in the Battle of Fredericksburg. It was not due to any shortcomings of the soldiers themselves, but rather to the fact that they were ordered, on that cold December morning in 1862, to charge uphill against Confederate troops who could stand and shoot from the safety of a sunken road. Over and over, Union General George Sykes ordered the attack. Each was brutally repelled until a sea of bleeding, groaning and dead bodies in blue lay before the Confederate line. From this sea of wounded came the cry, "Water! Water!" But any man who dared to set foot into that no-man's land would surely be killed.

Sergeant Richard Kirkland of the 2nd South Carolina Volunteers had heard all of the mournful cries that he could stand. Armed only with canteens of water and not permitted a flag of truce, the brave and mercy-filled sergeant slowly climbed over the stone wall that bordered the South's front line and stood there.

One hundred and fifty feet away men in blue who were angry, determined and feeling the sting of their loss, watched the lone, gray-clad figure. How many of those eyes were peering over the sight of a rifle will never be known.

Undeterred, Sgt. Kirkland approached the first wounded soldier, knelt by him, lifted his head and gave him a drink from a canteen. When he was done he rose and proceeded to the next man and did the same. Eyes of wonder, clad in both blue and gray, now watched transfixed as Kirkland hastened from man to fallen man administering the life giving liquid. For ninety minutes not a shot was fired, not a word called out. Finally, his mercy mission completed, the amazing Confederate sergeant returned to his lines, climbed back over the bullet-pocked stone wall and the killing resumed.

Sgt. Kirkland later survived the horror that was Gettysburg and was subsequently promoted to lieutenant. But at the Battle of Chickamauga, he was mortally wounded. Sergeant, Lieutenant, hero, call him what you wish. But following his selfless display of compassion at Fredericksburg, he will forever be known as "The Angel of Marye's Heights." Sometimes you don't **Fight on!**

The Wrong Man to Wrong

JAMES Brock left his native Ohio in the late 19th Century to make his fortune out west in the cattle business. He eventually got a small place on Foyle Creek in Texas and built up a herd. Since he also worked at the sutler's store in town, he needed help with his ranch and wrote to his two cousins in Ohio, Ed and Frank Woosley, to come and join him, which they did. He turned the running of the ranch over to the brothers.

In the spring of 1877, Frank Woosley went missing under mysterious circumstances. His brother suspected that Brock had murdered him. Brock was arrested and jailed to await trial. But the local Vigilante Committee decided to deal out swifter justice. That very night they rode for the jail to abduct and lynch Brock. But spring rains had swelled the creek between them and town and blocked their path. A few of the men, not really convinced of Brock's guilt, turned back for home. The rest, seeing they'd never get across the creek, finally did the same.

Brock, who had been proclaiming his innocence, went to trial. There wasn't enough evidence to convict him and he was acquitted and reluctantly released. He sold his half of the ranch to Ed Woosley and began a search for the "dead" Frank Woosley. He found that Woosley had passed through a cowboy camp shortly after his "death." He trailed his elusive cousin across several states, up into Canada and then down into Mexico.

The years passed with Frank Woosley always a step ahead of his pursuer. Then Brock got word his prey was living in Bald Knob, Arkansas. Brock beat a path to the man's door in Arkansas only to find he was not Woosley. Foiled once again, the downhearted Brock went to the station to catch the train back to Texas and there, in the station, he ran right into none other than his "dead" cousin, Frank Woosley. Brock pulled his pistol and threatened to make fiction into fact if Woosley tried to escape. The two then returned to Ohio, where family members, needing far less evidence than a Texas court, had long believed Brock guilty of murder.

Apparently, Ed and Frank had planned Frank's "murder" to frame Brock so they could get the ranch after he was hanged.

James Brock's search had lasted thirteen years and cost him all his money, but he cleared his name. **Don't Quit!**

"We've Got to Get Those Men"

(*Author's Note:* By mid-1967 the Johnson administration was expending ordinance (bombs) in Vietnam faster than it was replacing it. Thus they made a fateful decision. They ordered World War II vintage, 1,000 pound bombs, stored in the humid Philippine climate and manufactured in 1935, loaded onto the aircraft carrier, U.S.S. Forrestal, to be used by Navy aviators.

On the morning of July 29, 1967, while preparing for a strike on Vietnam, a missile slung beneath the wing of a Navy fighter aircraft on the starboard (right) side, received an electrical surge and launched without being manually fired. After passing through a sailor it struck an A-4 Skyhawk aircraft on the port (left) side of the ship, ripping it open and dumping hundreds of gallons of burning jet fuel onto the deck. The burning fuel engulfed other nearby aircraft adding their fuel to the inferno.

One minute and thirty-four seconds after the fire began, one of the old, inherently unstable, 1,000 pound bombs, which was engulfed by flames, exploded. Eight more would follow it. The massive explosions devastated the flight deck and those on it. Their explosions ripped even more airplanes open, disgorging their fuel to add to the fire. So powerful were the explosions that they blew debris downward through the entire ship and out the bottom causing the vessel to take on water. Burning fuel poured down these holes like water down a bathtub drain and ignited the aircraft in the hanger deck and throughout the many compartments below.

Many men sleeping in a berthing area on deck #2 beneath the flight deck and above the hanger deck were killed in their sleep, while others were horribly burned or mutilated. As the mighty ship listed to port by the water it was taking on, and blazed from the island back on all decks, some questioned if it could be saved.

Sailors fought a battle with flames that began shortly before 11AM and continued throughout the day and through the night. The devastated ship was saved due to the selfless gallantry which has become common among American fighting men. In all, 134 sailors lost their lives from the explosions, the fires, or in the effort to extinguish them.)

AS the fire and explosions racked the *U.S.S. Forrestal* on the morning of July 29, 1967, many sailors were blown completely off the ship and into the Gulf of Tonkin. Others, trapped by the flames, jumped into the gulf as it was their only way to escape a horrible death.

Throughout the battle a total of forty-seven men went overboard in various states of injury. Many were terribly burned and had no life preservers to help them stay afloat as the wounded ship left them behind, fighting valiantly for its own life.

When the fire began, David Clement was piloting a helicopter above the aircraft carrier. Whenever planes are launched or recovered, a helicopter hovers nearby to instantly rescue a pilot whose aircraft goes into the water for one reason or another. This morning that helicopter's call sign was *Angel 20* and Clement was its pilot.

On seeing the fire and initial explosion, Clement dove his craft to scan the wake of the ship. There he saw scores of burned and wounded sailors thrashing to stay afloat. "We have multiple men in the water, repeat, multiple men in the water!" he called over his radio as he requested assistance in retrieving them.

One by one, flitting and hovering like a dragonfly, *Angel 20* stopped above a thrashing figure in the sea and a rescue swimmer jumped in to aid the victim in coming aboard. As more men came on board, the overloaded helicopter had to work harder to hold its hover. Clement saw his engine temperature gauge hit the red line. It would seize at any time. Just as he spotted yet another injured sailor in the water, his flight controller on the nearby aircraft carrier, *Oriskany*, ordered him to break off his rescue attempts lest his engine quit and all on board should be lost. Clement looked at the *Oriskany* a mile away, then at his ever-climbing temperature gauge, then at the pitiful figure bobbing in the water who might not be there when he got back. "I can't leave them. We've got to get those men."

His swimmer helped him pluck the sailor from the water and Clement then scurried to the *Oriskany* and deplaned his human cargo. Then he was off again, hunting for more survivors. **Fight on!**

Not Now! Not Ever!

AS the *U.S.S. Forrestal* fought for its life against raging fires and exploding bombs on July 29, 1967, it was not alone. Several destroyers and two other aircraft carriers were cruising the waters of "Yankee Station" in the Gulf of Tonkin, using the area as a launch point for air strikes on North Vietnam. But these weren't the only war craft in the area. Since "Yankee Station" was located in international waters, numerous Vietnamese and even Chinese boats routinely shadowed the American fleet. Now, with the *Forrestal* preoccupied with survival and burning men leaping into the sea, this insidious fleet moved in like buzzards. There was a cash reward for any American prisoner they could capture and they aimed to take advantage of the situation.

Imagine leaping ninety feet from a carrier deck with your clothes ablaze, landing with second and third degree burns, only to be plucked from the water by a heartless enemy and spirited away right under the noses of your helpless countrymen. It simply was not going to happen.

As the enemy craft closed in on the helpless survivors, one of the accompanying American destroyers refused to allow them to spirit away any of the men. One of its five inch guns swung around and took aim on the offending but technically legal craft. The gun spoke once. One of the enemy boats literally disintegrated in the explosion that followed and the others turned and fled. Their evil designs were simply not going to be allowed. **Not now! Not ever!**

The Pigeon Counselor

AS if being cut off from their lines, low on rations, low on ammunition and completely surrounded by the Germans was not enough, the famous "Lost Battalion" of WWI also had the misfortune of being shelled by its own American artillery. As their position was being obliterated by friendly fire, the forlorn men released their last carrier pigeon with a desperate plea to cease fire. But the bird, Cher Ami, was overcome by the violence of the artillery barrage and the battle raging below. Confused by the fierce gunfire, she flew to a battle-denuded tree, and perched, refusing to leave regardless of encouragement and curses hurled by the doughboys, while German marksmen tried to bring her down. Hopeless eyes watched, waiting for the useless bird to be hit by a lucky German bullet.

Rather than curse, rather than hope, there was one young soldier that knew what needed to be done. While bullets whizzed by, he ran to the tree and climbed it. He edged out to the frightened bird, slowly grasped it and, ignoring the bullets the Germans were sending his way, softly stroked the terrified pigeon and spoke to it comfortingly. Finally, he tossed it into the air where it circled to get its bearing and then sped off and delivered the message that saved the battalion. **Fight on!**

(*Author's Note:* Cher Ami arrived less one eye and one leg, but she lived. She is now stuffed and on display in the Smithsonian Institute.)

Never Give Up, Never Give In

A young Texan named Babb had a small ranch near what is now Lubbock, Texas. He left his wife with their two small children, a year old baby and a family friend, a young widow that history identifies only as Lilly.

Babb had never had trouble with the Indians but that changed as soon as they knew he had left to drive some cattle north. Knowing the women were now defenseless, a band of Comanches swept in. First they scooped up the two young children playing at a nearby creek and then dashed into the house. They snatched the infant from its mother's arms and dashed it to the floor and then slit the young mother's throat. Then grasping Lilly and their other two captives, left the young wife for dead and rode off.

For days they rode giving nothing more than a little water to their captives. Lilly never did anything to stand out but all the time she watched and calculated. Finally, late one night, she stepped out of camp, lassoed one of the finest ponies, mounted it without either bridle or saddle and quietly walked the horse far from camp. Then she broke into a gallop and rode for her life.

For two days Lilly rode the empty prairie with neither food or water and only a trailing pack of hopeful wolves as company. Northward she rode ever looking over her shoulder.

Three days without sleep was too much. Lilly, with the end of the lasso tied around her arm, fell to the ground and fell into a deep sleep. The tethered animal grazed contentedly. Lilly woke up with a start to find herself surrounded by Indians. She had escaped the Comanches only to be captured by the Kiowas. Once again she was returned to Indian life. Once again she watched and waited. Once again she found herself quietly walking a recently lassoed pony away from camp in the dark of night. Once again she headed ever northward across a burning desolate desert, ever conscious of the fear behind.

The next day she drank the stinking, stagnant water she found in a buffalo wallow.

On her third desperate day of freedom she came to a wide Arkansas River. Knowing her only hope of safety lay beyond it, she forced her reluctant animal into the water. Shortly thereafter she glanced at the prairie at her feet and saw wagon ruts running to her left and right. With the fire of hope fully kindled, she scanned the horizon. She quickly discerned a wagon train headed her way from the east. The wagon master, Robert Bent, rode to meet her and then took her to a wagon where she was given food and water. Then Bent informed her that 15 miles east was the settlement of Big Turkey Creek, in Kansas. The gracious fellow offered to send an escort with her to the settlement. The young woman, full of pluck, declined the kind offer, mounted her stolen pony, blew her kindly benefactor a kiss and was off. She arrived at Big Turkey Creek having traveled over 500 miles from her point of origin.

The two Babb children were eventually ransomed and returned to their father. Lilly moved further east to Council Grove, Kansas, where she married and settled down. She had been captured but she never gave up and she never gave in. **Fight on!**

It Was Only Impossible

IT is impossible to land an A-1 Skyraider, a vintage World War II propeller driven fighter/bomber, on a runway only 2,500 feet long. It's even more impossible when that runway is pock-marked with mortar bomb craters, has fingers of torn steel pointing skyward that will shred an airplane's tires, has parts of a burning plane scattered all over it and is under enemy fire from both sides along its entire length.

Over 2,000 North Vietnamese Army troops were relentlessly attacking 368 nationals and 17 U.S. Army Green Berets in a U.S. Special Forces camp which the airstrip had served before being overrun by the NVA.

Four A-1E Skyraiders were supplying air support when one, piloted by U.S.A.F. Major Dafford W. Myers, was hit hard by groundfire. Trailing flames, Maj. Myers jettisoned everything but his centerline fuel tank, which refused to fall away, and headed for a gear-up landing at the strip. On contact with the ground Myer's fuel tank exploded and spewed burning wreckage onto the already debris riddled runway. Singed but not seriously injured, Myers leaped from the burning plane and hid in a nearby ditch. One of Myers' fellow pilots, and a good friend, Major Fisher, watched him crash land. Fisher called the Special Forces camp and asked the length of the runway. Thirty-five hundred feet. It would be tight but he could set the big Skyraider down in that distance. But he'd been misinformed. The runway was only 2,500 feet long, entirely too short to stop the plane after landing.

While the North Vietnamese filled the air with lead, Maj.

Fisher dropped onto the runway and stood on the brakes while maneuvering around craters, pieces of Myer's aircraft and other pieces of debris. As his overheated brakes faded, he shot off the end of the runway, crossed a small embankment and into a fuel storage area. He swung his plane around, hitting several 55 gallon drums with the tail, and taxied back to Myers. Maj. Myers jumped onto the wing, and Fisher pulled him head first into the cockpit and rammed the throttle wide open. While overhead three other A-1s, whose fuel was low and ammunition already spent, made low level passes on the NVA, Fisher danced his craft around obstacles and craters and willed it into the air.

Fisher landed at Pleiku with no less than 19 bullet holes. He was the first airman in the Vietnam War to be awarded the Medal of Honor. **Fight on!**

The Woman in His Life

WE never met her but we all know her name. Her wild-eyed son, Paul, wanted to be a pilot. The world was in the infancy of flight. Paul's dad wanted him to be a doctor; being a pilot was a foolish dream. But Paul's mother believed in him, believed in his dream. She encouraged him. He grew up and joined the fledgling United States Army Flier Corps. He became a pilot. He would retire years later a Brigadier General. He flew twenty-five harrowing missions over Europe in B-17s during WWII, but he's famous for only one. It wasn't in a B-17. It wasn't over Europe. It was in a B-29 Super Fortress. It was over Japan. It was August 6, 1945. Then Colonel Paul Tibbets, forever known as "The Man Who Won WWII," piloted his B-29 over Hiroshima, Japan, and dropped the world's first atomic bomb. He was piloting the airplane he had named for the woman who believed in him - his mother- *Enola Gay* - Enola Gay Tibbets.

Was it the vile, immoral act we've been told it was? Col. Tibbets didn't think so. He never regretted his actions. Neither did millions of men, both American and Japanese, who knew their lives would be up for grabs if an invasion of Japan had been necessary.

Millions of lives were saved. Peace came to the world, all because a mother believed in her son's dream. Don't be ashamed to **Fight on!**

"At the time we heard scuttlebutt that an invasion of Japan would be very costly in casualties...I thank Colonel Tibbetts and his crew, my wife Mary thanks them, our five children and fifteen grandchildren thank them."
(A Marine scheduled to invade Japan.)

"Had the dropping of the bomb not happened, I know that my husband would not have returned home - so many American lives would have been lost.

"My forty-six year old father was also in the Pacific....and my twenty year old brother was finishing flight training."
(A grateful wife, daughter, sister.)

"Hallelujah! Hallelujah!"
(Response of a naval officer destined for the invasion of Japan when he heard about the bombing of Hiroshima.)

"....in high school, I wrote a paper about why we shouldn't have dropped the [atomic] bomb on Hiroshima. I was adamant in my essay, but the moment I spoke with my grandfather, a Navy Seabee, and listened to his account of the war, I changed my mind.

"His blue eyes flared when I said the bomb was unnecessary, and he leaned across the table to tell me how the bomb had saved his life. How he was so grateful to go home and see his family again. How he's pretty sure he would have been killed otherwise. And so in a way, I realized I might not even be here if Paul Tibbets hadn't done his job."
(A formerly starry-eyed modern day high school girl.)

"...I was slated to head for the Pacific and fly cover for a land invasion of Japan...but thanks to the flight of the *Enola Gay*, the Army decided it didn't need me there after all....I left active duty that December [1945] a stateside-safeside WWII veteran."
(A B-29 navigator trainee in 1945)

"My husband was with the 5th Marine Division and served on Iwo Jima. After the *Enola Gay* dropped the bomb on Hiroshima, my husband and the men he fought with did not have to invade the Japanese mainland. He came home to me instead."
(The widow of a WWII veteran who died peaceably in his sleep, an old man, rather than on the beaches of Japan.)

"My wife and I have been married for fifty-two years. And I know in my heart why I have had the chance to do it. Because of what those men did....I just wanted to thank Paul Tibbets for letting me live my life."
(A seventy-four year old former WWII paratrooper.)

"He told Tibbets his father had said that had the war continued, 'all would have died'; that his father had said the end of the war spared the lives of 'men, women, children' all over Japan.

"I am very, very honored to have you here."
(The words of Shoji Tabuchi, Japanese entertainer, now U.S. citizen who stars in the Shoji Tabuchi Show in Branson, MO., when he met with Tibbets and the remaining Enola Gay *crewmen when they visited his show. Like Tibbets, as a child, Mr. Tabuchi also had a dream of coming to the United States and being an entertainer. A dream that could be fulfilled only because of the mission of Col. Paul Tibbets and the* Enola Gay.*)*

Fulfilling Her Responsibility

JOY Newmann and her friend were talking quietly on December 18, 1985, a summer day in Queensland, Australia, as they watched Joy's four children and their little friend Rosie playing a mere three feet away at the edge of Rock Creek, which fed out into the ocean. Suddenly, a large wave rose up, slapping the children down and dragging five-year-old Rosie out into the fast moving channel leading out into the sea. Momentarily stunned by the sudden wave, Joy came to herself and launched herself after the fast moving five-year-old, but the water drew the girl farther and farther away. After a frantic swim of 300 feet, she caught up with the terrified child. But now they were in mid channel and rapidly being swept out to sea. To make matters worse, the wind was picking up and waves were becoming aggressive.

Joy rolled onto her back, pulled Rosie on top of her and soothed her fears as she assured her someone would soon come for them. But thirty minutes passed before someone found a man with a small boat and headed him in their direction. The man searched blindly as he could see no one in the choppy water around him. Suddenly his boat dropped over a swell and almost on top of the couple. He grabbed Rosie and placed her in the boat as Joy passed out from exhaustion. But he managed to wrestle the brave woman into the boat. She hadn't forgotten her responsibility to take care of her children's friend. **Fight on!**

Desperate Relay

RALPH Border was hunting Dall sheep 60 miles southeast of Fairbanks, Alaska, with his brother-in-law, Bill Gonce, when a 500 pound sow and her two 400 pound cubs attacked them. The sow rocketed down the slope they were on, grabbed Border by the arm and then lost her footing and the two of them tumbled down hill coming to rest 80 feet below where the attack started. While Bill drove off the cubs with his 30.06 rifle, the grizzly began chewing on Border's arm, leg and face.

Free of the cubs, Gonce put three shots in the bear, killing it, but not before it had horribly mauled his brother-in-law. The men were five miles from their cabin and it was 4 PM. Spurred by the desperate circumstances, they covered the five miles in a mere hour. When they arrived they found the packer in camp. He immediately hoisted Border onto his horse and ran two miles, leading the horse to another sheep hunter's cabin. The only hope of getting Border out alive was to call for a medevac over the radio-telephone located at a gold mine cabin nine miles away. Leroy Sewell, one of the hunters and a native of the area, immediately took off running through the almost knee-deep snow to where he knew a three-wheeled ATV was cached. He then rode to the cabin where miner Pat Peede called for a helicopter to pick Border up. The helicopter sent was on maneuvers at Fort Greely and headed straight for the injured man without refueling. Once onboard they headed for Fort Greely. But between the helicopter and help was a vicious snow squall. With his fuel gauge on empty, the pilot was advised to fly around the storm. He couldn't. There wasn't enough fuel. He was then advised to climb to 2,500 feet to fly over it. No can do. As he waited to hear his engine quit, the pilot did the only thing he could do: He thrust his fragile ship right into the storm. The helicopter pitched and jumped but kept flying and landed at the base hospital where emergency crews took over and raced Border into surgery.

By spring, Border, the subject of numerous plastic surgeries, was back out hunting....bear. Fight on!

An Appointment With Destiny

ON July 9, 1755, during the French and Indian War, a force of over 1,300 British Regulars under command of General Edward Braddock was marching to launch an attack on the French Fort Duquesne (now Pittsburgh). Seven miles from their objective they marched right into a French and Indian ambush. Firing from behind trees and bushes they decimated their red-coated rivals who stood by ranks and fired blindly at their invisible enemy. Bullet after bullet slammed into the helpless, panic stricken British soldiers who broke and ran, leaving cannon, guns, wagons, baggage, provisions and 25,000 British pounds. More than half their men lay dead or dying. Singled out by the Indians, every mounted officer was killed except one, a twenty-three year old colonial named George Washington. Twice his horse was shot from under him, and he sustained four bullet holes in his coat but was miraculously unhurt.

Fifteen years later, in 1770, Washington was exploring in Ohio country. An old Indian chief, hearing he was in the territory, traveled many miles to meet the man all the Indians believed to be protected by God. Referring back to the slaughter fifteen years earlier, he told all in attendance the instructions he had given his warriors and the result. Pointing to Washington, who had been everywhere on the battlefield carrying Braddock's orders and trying to rally the men, he said, "Quick, let your aim be certain, and he dies. Our rifles were leveled, rifles which, but for you, knew not how to miss - 'twas all in vain; a power mightier far than we shielded you. Seeing you were under the special guardianship of the Great Spirit, we immediately ceased to fire at you. I am old and soon shall be gathered to the great council fire of my fathers in the land of shades; but ere I go, there is something bids me speak in the voice of prophecy. Listen! The Great Spirit protects that man [pointing at Washington], and guides his destinies - he will become the chief of nations, and a people yet unborn will hail him as the founder of a mighty empire. I am come to pay homage to the man who is the particular favorite of Heaven and who can never die in battle."

"Safety is of the Lord."

Aggressive at All Times

WHEN World War II broke out, mild-mannered Freddie Tilston left his job in Windsor, Ontario, at the Sterling Drugs Company, joined the Canadian Army and soon became an officer.

In March of 1945, his 2nd Canadian Division soldiers were slugging it out with desperate, battle-hardened German troops in the Hochwald Forest. Major Tilston led his men courageously during the battle. Although he had an eye shot out and a wound in the hip, he fearlessly crossed an open field to get more ammunition for his men while German fire attempted to end his heroic effort. He made the trip six times.

Finally, a mortar round hit near him and both of his legs were mangled. He refused medical evacuation until German resistance ended. As a result of his wounds, both of his legs had to be amputated. But that wouldn't stop this charging Canadian.

He returned to his job at Sterling Drugs on artificial legs. Ever aggressive, he was soon appointed Vice President of Sales. He then went on to become the company President. Not one to stop while an objective remained unsecured, he ended his tenure at Sterling as Chairman of the Board.

In war and peace Freddie Tilson had learned the value of being aggressive. **Fight on!**

How the West Was Won

WHEN it came to the problem of taming the Wild West, few would expect the answer to come from a lowly "laughing gas" salesman in New England, but it did.

Sam started his career at age 10 working in his father's silk mill in Hartford, Connecticut. He endured only two years of formal education before abandoning that for a life at sea. While studying the ship's windless he came up with the idea for an invention. He developed two working models of his invention. One didn't work and the other exploded. Having failed at inventing, he turned to selling nitrous oxide. For three years he toured the country selling citizens on the benefits of a dose of his "laughing gas" to lift their spirits. Still possessed with his little invention, he pursued numerous wealthy citizens to invest in its manufacture, only to see business fail. He went bankrupt.

Not one to give up, Sam made some improvements to his invention. In the mid 1800's, parties in Texas learned of it and Sam's success was guaranteed. The Texas Rangers purchased the "Colt Repeating Pistol" and Samuel P. Colt became the source of the weapon that tamed the West. **Fight on!**

A Cry in the Night

(*Author's Note*: During the winter of 1981 a brutal Arctic storm reached down into the Gulf of Alaska and ravaged the fishing vessel, *St. Patrick*. One massive wave destroyed the wheelhouse, shorted out the electrical system and stopped the engine. Before the beleaguered ship could sink beneath them, the thirteen crewmen hastily donned their survival suits and abandoned ship. Eleven of them leaped into the brutally cold water from the stern. Only one of these, Wallace Thomas, would survive. His story was told in *Fight On!*, "The Breath of Life." The remaining two jumped from the bow. Only one of these, Bob Kidd, survived. This is his harrowing tale.)

BOB Kidd and his good friend, Doc Steigel, leaped into the frigid waters of the Gulf of Alaska in the wee hours of November 30, 1981. Steigel's suit began to leak and the icy waters quickly sapped his strength. Waves continually battered and then separated the two. Finally, after one grievous monster-wave, Kidd lost contact with his friend for good. Now he was on his own. Without the company of his friend, who was much stronger than he, Kidd felt hopelessness seize upon him. He wept in despair in the cold waters. Then he turned his face to the dark heavens and called to the only One who can hear such cries, "I don't want to die! I don't want to die!" Shortly thereafter he felt his resolve return. He determined to fight for life as long as he could. He managed to pull his arms and legs up into the survival suit and roll into a ball to conserve body heat. Then from a wave top he spied Afognak Island. He called out, "Oh, thank you, God. Thank you, God," and then assured himself, "If I can see it, I can get to it." He put his arms and legs back into his suit and started swimming.

Many tired hours later Bob Kidd reached the island only

to become trapped in the surf that was dashing against the fifteen hundred foot cliff at its edge. His leaking survival suit had filled with frigid water, and he was helpless in the boiling surf. Kidd wrestled the waterlogged suit off and managed to pull himself onto the rocks where the violent waves now threatened to crush him. He had only one recourse. He would have to climb the cliff face or die. The temperature was 20 degrees and twenty knot winds tried to peel him off the cliff. After hours of grueling climbing, Kidd made it to the top. His helpless situation had been punctuated by a U.S. Coast Guard helicopter which had flown by without seeing him.

Once on top, Kidd set off hoping to find a hunter's cabin. His frozen feet were like two clubs. When night fell, he climbed into a hole made by the root system of a fallen tree and slept.

The next day he made his way down to a beach area to discover a small navy of vessels searching for him. A helicopter spotted him, zoomed in and whisked him to a waiting Coast Guard cutter. From there it was to the hospital. With a body temperature of only 81 degrees, he was in critical condition. But he had fought for life and won. **Fight on!**

(*Author's Note*: Eleven out of thirteen people perished when they abandoned the *St. Patrick*. Possibly none of them had to. She never sank. The day after she was abandoned, she was found adrift by some fishing boats and towed into port. **Hang on!**)

He Refused to Get Bitter

TO lose a leg at the young age of 18 can make a young man bitter. It happened to Confederate private James E. Hanger - and made him rich.

Pvt. Hanger lost his leg to a Union cannonball at Philippi, Virginia. But his life was saved by a Union surgeon of the 16th Ohio Regiment who amputated the young man's shattered leg just below the hip. While recuperating, Hanger used his pocket knife to fashion an artificial leg out of some barrel staves. He did such a good job that he was soon producing artificial legs for other amputees.

The Civil War ended and the former Confederate private founded the J.E. Hanger Company of Richmond, Virginia., to produce artificial limbs for war survivors. By the time he died in 1919, his company had branches in four U.S. cities as well as London and Paris. **Fight on!**

He Walked Home

THE letters "PJ" are short for pararescuemen. Their job used to involve parachuting in to help downed airmen, thus "PJ" for "pararescue jumper." Today they almost always ride in on helicopters to make their rescues. Although they are Air Force personnel, they are called on to rescue Army Special Forces, Navy SEALS, and Marine Force Recon as well as Air Force personnel. They take their motto, *"That Others May Live,"* very seriously. They will hazard their own lives to save someone else. The story is told of a PJ assigned to a Huey UH-1 in Vietnam. They went in to pull out a special forces patrol. Once the helicopter was loaded it was too heavy to get airborne. So, *"That Others May Live,"* the PJ simply jumped off the helicopter and waved it away. He then proceeded to walk back to friendly territory. It took him six days. **Fight on!**

"Better than anything to eat; better than anything to drink; better than anything in the world."

(Gold miner Elie Ritchott describing fresh air after being trapped in a cave in for thirty-six hours.)

Better Than Anything

IN 1880, gold miner Elie Ritchott, sank a shaft straight down in what was then Montana Territory. At 42 feet he hit an old streambed and found gold among the gravel of the stream. He then dug a low 200 foot long horizontal shaft along the stream bed.

He was in the horizontal shaft one day when it caved in between him and the vertical shaft leading to safety. Sixty feet back the shaft was blocked solid. Assuming the entire shaft was caved in, Ritchott knew there was no hope of clearing the unstable shaft. Neither was there hope that anyone would happen by his mine, descend the vertical shaft and dig him out. But Ritchott wasn't one to give up. He was a miner and digging is what miners do. So with the flickering light of a candle, he began a tunnel that angled toward the surface. For hours he dug, breaking rock out ahead of him and scooting it behind him with his feet. After fourteen hours of digging, Ritchott broke into a large chamber formed when his tunnel had collapsed. Four hours later his last candle burned out, so the miner worked on in total darkness.

More than a day had passed since the cave-in when the weakening miner's crowbar struck a roof timber in his original shaft. Several more hours passed before he pried the timber enough to smell fresh air for the first time in almost 30 hours. He finally dropped to the floor of his shaft, crawled to the ladder and gazed up at blue sky 42 feet above. He gathered his strength and forced himself up the ladder emerging back on the surface almost 36 hours after the cave-in. **Fight on!**

Forced Mountain Landing

ON Feb. 16, 2002, 1st Lt. Thomas Cahill was the pilot of an HH-60-G. Lt. Cahill was flight lead for a pair of PAVE Hawks that were being ferried from Kandahar Afghanistan to Karshi-Khanabad (K-2) airbase in Uzbekistan. The flight would require them to thread their way through the Hindu Kush mountains. They would be flying between mountains at an altitude of 11,000 feet while actually only about 500 feet above the ground. At that altitude the PAVE Hawk is at its extreme altitude limit and just barely able to maintain flight. The twin-engine workhorse is barely flying and has no reserve power.

As they flew over the mountains, they flew right into a fierce snowstorm. Suddenly the digital electronic control fuel unit malfunctioned on engine one and the turbine lost power. Being only 500 feet above the mountains they would hit the side of a mountain in just four seconds. In that minuscule time period before impact, Captain Ed Lengel, another flight lead qualified pilot, who was flying as Cahill's copilot that day because he needed a ride to K-2, reached to the console overhead and did a manual override on the DEC of engine one. The engine surged to life. That brief surge of power helped Cahill clear a large boulder and aim for a small patch of snow on the side of a mountain at a 30 degree nose up angle. The rotor flexed down and tore an unhealthy portion off the tips of all four blades.

Four feet behind the helicopter was a sheer cliff with a 2000 foot drop-off. The PAVE Hawk began sliding backwards down the slope towards the drop-off. A crewman in back mashed the intercom and yelled "Power, power, power. We're sliding back." The rear stabilator slid out into the thin air. Lt. Cahill pulled full power and added forward cyclic, an action that tilts the rotors down in front for forward flight. The rotor leaned down and beat into the 15 feet of snow. He was literally "flying" the helicopter into the side of the mountain. Rearward movement was arrested with the tail wheel a foot from the edge of the cliff. They had no radio contact with their sister ship. An air rescue would have been impossible and if Cahill shut down the engine the helicopter would simply slide backward off the mountain. They had only one chance. Lt. Cahill decided to try to fly the helicopter off the mountain. But at that altitude, with six men aboard, the overworked HH-60-G wouldn't even hover a foot off the ground. They needed to lighten the ship. The helicopter had about 2,900 pounds of fuel in its fuel tanks. They would have to drop 1900 pounds to even hope to hover. Fumes from the exiting fuel filled the cabin. Cahill instructed his crew that if a fire broke out, they were to dive out of the helicopter. Then he planned to cut power and ride the burning craft backwards over the cliff. He figured losing one life was better than losing six. No fire started, but neither did the helicopter fly. Still too heavy. Out went 500 more pounds of fuel. Then out went all the weight they could lose. Lt Cahill needed to turn the craft 90 degrees and launch it off the cliff. But the tail rotor was too close to a rock formation to do that. What to do?

What Lt. Cahill did was "hop" the HH-60-G up the mountainside to a spot 40 feet above them where he had room to maneuver. He turned the battered helicopter around, facing into a zero visibility blizzard, and, after a brief roll launched it off the cliff. The damaged rotors bit into the thin air and the PAVE Hawk wobbled into the air. After an equally danger-filled return flight, the two helicopters landed at Bagram air base. **Fight on!**

Foot Race on the Ocean Floor

THE NR-1 was a submarine like no other. Built in the 60's it is only 135 feet long and just over 12 feet wide. It had a crew of just 12 men. But unique to it are the viewing windows in the nose, the robotic grapling arm and wheels. Yes, wheels. Located on the centerline in bicycle fashion, are two retractable large rubber tires that allow the NR-1 to "drive" along the sea bottom. The NR-1 possessed no weapons whatsoever. No torpedoes. No missiles. Nothing. It was not built as a weapon. Rather the U.S. Navy used it (uses, it is still in service) for research and clandestine operations. It has been in active service since June 18, 1970.

Prior to going into active service - it has never been officially commissioned - NR-1 underwent undersea trials off the U.S. east coast. In November of 1969, such a sea trial almost brought about the loss of the NR-1 with all hands. The little submarine was rolling along the floor of the Atlantic Ocean in a deep water area known as Baltimore Canyon. After extending its wheels and gently settling on the bottom, the crew pumped extra water into the ballast tanks to hold the craft on the ocean floor while it "drove" along the bottom at about one knot per hour. As it traveled along, the strange craft began to descend a gentle slope. But it was unnatural for the sub to operate in anything but a level attitude. So a crew member pumped even more water into the front ballast tank until the nose finally settled. Down the slope they went. Suddenly, the crew member who was laying on his stomach gazing out of the viewing port in the lower half of the nose screamed an alarm. "Go back! Go back! We're going over the edge!" Suddenly the sub slipped over the lip of an uncharted undersea canyon and drifted relentlessly down into the darkness. Dropping nose first the forward-looking sonar detected no bottom. The captain was afraid to initiate an "Emergency Blow" of the ballast tanks because he was afraid they may ascend under an undersea shelf in the narrow canyon and cause a seaslide that would bury them. Finally, as the depth gauge hit 3000 feet - the NR-1's test depth - the little sub slammed into the ocean floor, crushing the door for the robotic arm and settling into the thick mud at the bottom.

The NR-1's design incorporated thrusters both fore and aft to help position the boat. The thrusters were engaged full up but the sticky mud held the little craft fast. They had no communication with the surface, not that it could have helped. The tiny sub had only one hatch, in the floor of the conning tower. There was no way for a deep submersible rescue vessel to attach to it. The men were on their own.

It was decided to pump a limited amount of water out of the ballast tanks to try to tear the boat loose from the bottom without triggering a landslide. For hours the pumps eased the water out of the tanks. Nothing changed, they remained fast on the bottom. All seemed hopeless. Then the captain had an idea. He instructed the six off duty crewmen to go to the rearmost part of the boat while he pumped water from the front trim tank to the rear one, while applying full power to two forward thrust motors hoping to pry the bow out of the mud. Then on his command they all rushed forward while the process was reversed. Back and forth the men rushed while the front and rear thrusters screamed. Finally, the man lying on his stomach saw the mud move against the glass. "We're moving!" With huge sheets of mud clinging to its hull, the NR-1 slowly rose a few feet above the ocean floor and was gingerly guided out of the deep ocean valley and back to the surface. **Fight on!**

"You know my love, we have to do this. That's the only way to get out of here. I have no other choice."

Luis Grass, heroic Cuban refugee

The Hunger for Freedom

AT 3:00 on the morning of July 15, 2003, Luis Grass, a citizen of Havana, Cuba, got in his 1951 Chevy truck with his family and several friends, and drove into the waters of the Florida Strait. Were they fulfilling some bizarre suicide pact? No. They were a dozen Cubans yearning for freedom in America and hoping to get there by sailing Grass's truck which he had converted into a makeshift boat. (It is illegal to own a boat in this "Worker's Paradise.") Forty miles from the Florida coast they were intercepted by the U.S. Coast Guard, taken onboard and their truck sunk by gunfire. They were returned to Cuba and faced much grief from its Communist government.

No problem! Luis simply converted a 1959 Buick Electra into a boat and, with twelve aboard, made the plunge again on February 2, 2004. Just ten miles from the Florida coast they were again stopped by the Coast Guard. Grass' passengers were returned to Cuba while Grass, his wife and four year old son were granted refugee status in Costa Rica. But Costa Rica isn't the United States. In early 2005, he and his family began hitchhiking the 2,100 miles to the U.S./Mexican border. They crossed Nicaragua, Honduras, Guatemala and Mexico arriving in Brownsville, Texas, in March where he promptly applied for political asylum. It was granted. **Fight on!**

(*Author's Note:* Rafael Diaz was one of those aboard Grass' 59 Buick and sent back to Cuba. On June 5, 2005, he and eleven other freedom-hungry Cubans loaded into a 1948 Mercury "boat" and "drove" due north. Just short of Florida they too were intercepted and their vehicle sunk. But since the Diaz family had already arranged U.S. visas, they were allowed into the United States.)

Ole #1124's Last Run

ON May 31, 1889, the South Fork Dam, 14 miles north of Johnstown, Pennsylvania, disintegrated during torrential spring rains. Before slamming into Johnstown and taking over 2,200 lives, the raging waters barreled down the Conemaugh River gorge and obliterated the tiny burgs of South Fork, Mineral Point, East Conemaugh and Woodvale.

Engineer John Hess had boarded engine #1124 and headed north out of East Conemaugh that day. Word was that there was a track washout near Mineral Point. He had no way of knowing that just minutes earlier the South Fork Reservoir had burst through the earthen dam and wiped the community of South Fork off the map. Twenty million gallons of angry, boiling water were headed for Mineral Point. Hess' locomotive and the waters were on a collision course.

South of Mineral Point, Hess and his crew were inspecting track damage when an ungodly roar from the north filled their ears. Upriver the waters were heading directly west before following the riverbed south. The men looked north and saw trees bending over and disappearing as though an invisible giant was brushing them aside as he walked. Then the giant exploded around the bend and headed south, rolling trees, mud and debris before it. Every man cried out and raced for the safety of the hillsides just yards away. Every man but John Hess. With a glance south toward East Conemaugh, Hess thought of the hundreds there who were about to be visited by watery death without warning. NO! It would not be without warning. Hess sprinted to the cab of his steam engine, lashed the whistle wide open and threw the engine into reverse as the waters chased him down the tracks.

A locomotive whistle tied wide open means one thing; disaster. When the people of East Conemaugh heard Hess' whistle and saw his train barreling backwards toward town, they instantly guessed at just what the disaster was.

"The dam's broke!", "To high ground," came the cries. As they ran, they saw the 40 foot high mass of boiling, churning liquid death closing on Hess' engine.

His duty done, Hess threw on the brakes, leaped from the engine and scampered up the hillside. He turned and watched as the violent waters slammed into his train, lifting it from the tracks and tumbling it into town.

Hundreds of people lived that day because of the selfless action of one man. **Fight on!**

(*Author's Note:* The churning waters of the Johnstown Flood were so powerful, and the devastation so hideous, that bodies from Johnstown were still being found in 1911, twenty-two years later, some as far away as Cincinnati, Ohio.)

Not My Plane, You Don't!

(Author's Note: All pilots guard their airplanes jealously, missionary pilots more so because they realize the important service their aircraft provides.)

J.T. Lyons, a missionary pilot with Baptist Mid-Missions in Liberia in the late 1960's, had just coasted his bright red Piper Super Cub to a stop in the town of Yila. Nearby a wild bull saw the red airplane and charged toward it. Missionary Lyons was not about to have the Lord's property damaged by a rampaging bull. Fearlessly he leaped from the pilot's seat, rushed between the airplane and the animal and raised his fists, prepared to defend his plane barehanded. The startled animal stopped, pawed the ground and lowered his head for the final charge. The defiant Baptist Missionary, determination blazing in his eyes, stood his ground. The two antagonists stared at each other for what seemed like an eternity. Then the buffaloed bull snorted, turned and walked off. **Fight on!**

The Cannon That Changed History

ON August 12, 1914, the army of Austria invaded Serbia at several points along its western border. Slowly the Serbians fell back, putting up a stiff resistance, while two of the Austrian army groups moved to unite and then drive into the heart of Serbia.

Between these converging Austrian armies was the Serbian 4th Artillery Regiment which was pulling back from being cut off by the northern movement of the southernmost Austrian army. All seemed lost. Then one Major Djukitch of the 4th Artillery Regiment asked permission to take just one cannon and resist the southern Austrian army. Permission was granted. Djukitch set up his lone cannon directly in the path of the Austrian onslaught. When the vanguard came into view, he opened fire. Instead of quickly overwhelming the lone gun, the Serbian force broke and ran.

Thirty minutes into the amazing battle, Major Djukitch received orders to cease fire and pull back. Instead, the daring major sent back word of his startling success and requested to be reinforced with artillery, infantry and cavalry. They were sent. The resulting battle drove the Austrians from the field and ultimately doomed their invasion of Serbia. **Fight on!**

"Shell and Be Damned!"

FOLLOWING the Civil War battle of Shepherdstown, Virginia, on October 1, 1862, there were numerous dead and wounded Union soldiers scattered on the battlefield under Confederate guns. In such cases, a flag of truce would be shown by one of the sides and both armies would consent to allow the other to collect its casualties. No such flag had been displayed. The cries of the wounded stirred the heart of a Union soldier, Lt. Lemuel L. Crocker, to request permission of his commanding officer to go out and retrieve the helpless men. His commanding officer passed the request on to General Fitz-John Porter who coldly denied the request. But that didn't stop the wounded from bleeding and pleading. Nor did it settle the troubled heart of Lt. Crocker. In blatant disregard of the denial, the lieutenant crossed the Potomac River on an earthen dam, (fully-armed.) Under full view of both armies, Crocker began to carry his wounded comrades to the bank of the river.

Suddenly, an orderly sent by General Porter, called to him that he was to return immediately or he would order the artillery to shell him. Incredulous at the general's heartlessness and totally unimpressed by the threat, Crocker called out, "Shell and be damned!" and returned to his mission of mercy.

As Crocker continued his mission, a Confederate general and his staff rode up. They wished to know what he was doing, why he was armed and why there was no flag of truce displayed. Crocker, covered with the blood of the wounded, informed the general in no uncertain terms that, regardless of the rules of war, his commander's refusal or Confederate interference, he was there to return the bodies and the wounded to their rightful place at home.

The general asked how long Crocker had been in the service.

"Twenty days."

With that, the general pointed to a boat Crocker could use to carry his charges across the river and then set a picket of guards around the area to assure he wasn't molested.

The intrepid lieutenant loaded the boat, crossed the river, and was immediately arrested.

But who could condemn such a brave and selfless act? After a tongue-lashing and a crash course on military protocol, the brave and compassionate lieutenant was released. **Fight on!**

> "I thought: You dirty bird. You're not going to get him without fighting me to the very end."
>
> — *Lorraine Lengkeek*

Because She Didn't Have Her Purse

DEANE and Lorraine Lengkeek of Holland, Michigan, were hiking to Iceberg Lake in Glacier National Park on August 30, 1991, when a sow bear with two cubs attacked them. The beast charged into Deane and bit him in the shoulder, arm and chest. Before the attack happened, Lorraine, a 62 year old grandmother with fifteen grandchildren, had been musing over the beauty around her and singing the hymn, "How Great Thou Art." Now she was watching a mad grizzly bear savaging the man with whom she had spent most of her life. This would never do! The only weapon Lorraine had was the binoculars she was carrying around her neck. The 5' 4", 130 lb. wife and grandmother took the binoculars by the strap and in a defensive rage swung them, smashing them down on the bear's head. The stunned brute looked up at the fire in the little lady's eyes and bolted. Deane was helicoptered to the hospital and survived. **Fight on!**

Our Song

ON September 13, 1814, after British Army had burned Washington D.C., they were poised to occupy Baltimore. But Fort McHenry stood in their way. That night sixteen British ships lobbed between 1,500 and 1,800 shells down on the one thousand defenders within the fort's walls.

American Commander Major George Armistead had ordered his troops to fly "a flag so large that the British will have no difficulty in seeing it from a distance."

All night long the bombardment mercilessly hammered away at the fort's walls. But in the morning our flag still waved, the fort still stood and the stunned British ships sailed off. Only four Americans had been killed. The fort had held.

Aboard one British ship, Francis Scott Key was retrieving a friend and other prisoners who the British were exchanging. But the British had forced him to stay aboard ship until they mounted the night's attack. Overwhelmed with emotion, Key watched the battle through the night. The next morning he viewed his flag still defiantly flying. He immortalized the American tenacity he had witnessed with a poem entitled "The Star Spangled Banner." It was only fitting it would become our nation's anthem. **They fought on.**

"Does not such a country, and such defenders of their country, deserve a song?"

Francis Scott Key

He'd Had Enough

AIR Force Major, George E. "Bud" Day, was shot down over North Vietnam and taken prisoner on August 25, 1967. During his five years of captivity, Maj. Day was continuously and mercilessly tortured by his captors. Sometimes it was in hopes of getting useful military information, which he never gave. Sometimes it was simply because of the blood hatred Communists have for America. While CBS was reporting that American POWs were being treated well, Bud Day was being tortured. While Jane Fonda was laughing it up with his tormentors, Bud Day was being tortured. But one a day in 1970, Bud Day finally had enough.

Day and numerous other prisoners decided to have a Bible-oriented church service. The North Vietnamese guards ordered it stopped. The prisoners continued their sacred worship. Later, guards came and yanked several prisoners out of the service. This interference with Divine service "flipped" Day's switch. He stood and began defiantly singing *The Star Spangled Banner*. The entire camp joined in. For two hours the battered, beaten, tormented Americans sang every patriotic song they could. The cowed Vietnamese backed down.

Major Bud Day was returned to the U.S. in March of 1973. He served until his retirement in 1976 at the rank of Colonel. In addition to the Medal of Honor, he received the Air Force Cross, the Distinguished Service Medal and the Silver Star. He holds almost seventy military decorations, making him the most decorated Air Force officer in history. **Fight on!**

Fake It!

ONE dark night in the early 1860's, Joseph Wirtle, while riding for the Pony Express, rode unexpectedly right into an Indian camp. He knew he had to act fast or he was a dead man. He couldn't turn and try to leave or the Indians would have killed him. So, acting as though he belonged there, Wirtle reigned up, dismounted, handed his reins to a warrior who happened to be standing there and sauntered into a nearby lodge. A little later he strolled back out, handed the warrior a gift, mounted his horse and rode off. **Fight on!**

An Audacious Escape

COLDITZ Castle in the German town of the same name was the most foreboding of German prisoner of war camps of World War II. In attempting to escape, many dug tunnels and some even sought to fly out over its walls. But six imaginative inmates found a unique, as well as audacious, manner of escaping.

One morning, after much planning and preliminary preparations, six POW's, tunneled into a storeroom. Moments later they stepped outside, four dressed as POW's from a nearby camp which sent over temporary workers from time to time; the other two were dressed as German guards. Then they boldly walked right out through the gate. A German guard even held the gate open for them. **Fight on!**

Say It Ain't So

FRANCIS Gabreski wanted to be a pilot more than anything in the world. So it hurt him deeply that day in 1938 when his private flight instructor told him he didn't have "the touch" to be a pilot.

When Germany invaded Poland in 1939, the home of Gabreski's ancestors, he joined the Army Air Corps and again tried flying. His instructor was unimpressed with his flying skills and recommended him for an elimination flight that would send him to the infantry.

But Gabreski was determined to fly. He squeaked past his elimination flight and made it to the ranks of fighter pilot. It as a good thing, too. He went to Europe and shot down 28 German aircraft. He finished the war as America's top ace.

Gabreski next flew jets in the Korean War where he recorded an additional 6.5 victories. Thirty-four and a half victories for a man who was told twice he didn't have what it took to be a pilot. His determination wrote a different destiny. **Fight on!**

Fight On...and On...and On!

PRENTISS Ingraham, son of Rev. John Holt Ingraham, was born in Natchez, Mississippi, in 1843. Before he turned twenty, the Civil War had begun and Ingraham joined the Confederate Army. When that war ended, Ingraham went to Mexico and helped Benito Juarez oust Emperor Maxmillian. No more fighting there so he sailed to Europe and fought in the Austro-Prussian Seven Weeks War of 1866. Let's see, where to next? Ah yes, Crete! Here, he fought with the Greeks against the Turks. With Europe now solvent, Ingraham sailed back to his side of the world to fight with Cuban rebels against the Spanish. In Cuba, Ingraham was captured by the Spanish and condemned to death. But somehow, rather than dying, he next showed up in the American West as a sidekick to none other than Buffalo Bill Cody.

Finally, Ingraham retired from a soldier's life and settled down to write. And write he did. He attacked writing like it was an enemy bastion needing to be conquered. For the next 34 years he wrote an average of 1,350,000 words per year. Without a computer or word processor he averaged over 3,700 words an hour - 154 words per minute.

Writing under pseudonyms such as "Dr. Noel Dunbar," "Midshipman Tom W. Hall" and "Dangerfield Burr," he pumped out novels. It was he who immortalized Buffalo Bill Cody and formed America's idea of what the wild west was like. By the time he died in 1904, he had published almost one thousand novels and novelettes. **Get Busy!**

The Other Six-Day War

FOR six days in June of 1967 the nation of Israel fought one of its numerous wars of survival in what became a stunning victory over its Arab neighbors. It wasn't their first and wouldn't be their last. This miraculous June, 1967, victory became known as "The Six Day War."

The modern nation of Israel became a nation again on May 14, 1948. The very next day she was attacked by forces from Trans-Jordan, Syria, Lebanon, and Iraq. It was a war with the goal of exterminating the infant nation.

Egypt, attacking from Gaza in the south, could reach Israel's capital in just one day. With that, the war would be over, and Israel would cease to exist. But about a mile from the Egyptian Army's jumping off point was the isolated Kibbutz *Yad Mordechai*.

Occupied by only 135 people, *Yad Mordechai* was situated on the road to Tel Aviv. The Egyptians could not bypass it. The tiny Jewish settlement faced the wrath of an entire Egyptian brigade of about 5,000 men, backed by artillery, armored cars, tanks and even aircraft. It was to be a mere hiccup on the way to Tel Aviv and victory.

The Egyptian attack began on May 18 when aircraft bombed and strafed the kibbutz. The next day they dropped incendiary bombs while Egyptian artillery opened up. Then came an infantry attack on an Israeli pillbox manned by just seven men. The vastly outnumbered defenders waited patiently until they knew their limited ammunition could be used to its full effect. Then they let loose. Sharpshooters took out Egyptian officers while automatic fire devastated the ranks. The attack disintegrated. Two more times the Egyptians threw themselves at the tiny pillbox. Each time they were thrown back. Direct artillery fire hammered the structure, but the resolute Jewish defenders held out until their ammunition was expended. Then they faded back to the kibbutz and took a place among the regular defenders.

The kibbutz now felt the full force of the Egyptian onslaught. But as waves of Egyptian infantry swarmed in, determined Jewish fire thinned their ranks and stalled their efforts.

Over the next six days, Egyptians died by the hundreds attempting to conquer the tiny settlement. Finally, on May 23 came the tanks, with their ammunition gone, and no ability to stop armor, the kibbutz was at last evacuated.

But the six days had sapped the attacker's will to fight as well as depleted their ranks. More than that it gave the young nation of Israel six days to purchase desperately needed arms. The Egyptian column that finally overran Kibbutz *Yad Mordechai* headed for Tel Aviv only to be shattered by Israeli aircraft purchased while *Yad Mordechai* was holding out against its attackers. Tel Aviv would not fall. Israel would survive because of a six day battle that decided the fate of a nation. **Fight on!**

Now these are the nations which the LORD left, to prove Israel by them, even as many of Israel as had not known all the wars of Canaan;

Only that the generations of the children of Israel might know, to teach them war, at the least such as before knew nothing thereof;

Judges 3:1, 2

So let all thine enemies perish, O LORD: but let them that love him be as the sun when he goeth forth in his might. And the land had rest forty years.

Judges 5:31

The Lady Was "Unsinkable"

THE *Titanic* was the second of three Olympic class ocean liners built for the White Star Line, the first being the *Olympic*, for which the class was named, and the third, the *Brittannic*. Amazingly, one woman sailed on all three and was involved in a shipwreck on each one.

The *Olympic* - Violet Jessop was part of the ship's staff when, on September 20, 1911, the speed of the great liner created such a suction as it passed the British cruiser, *HMS Hawke*, that the smaller cruiser was drawn irresistibly into the side of the liner. Both were damaged. Neither sank.

The *Titanic* - Violet Jessop was also part of the ship's crew when this great liner struck an iceberg on its maiden voyage and sank in the North Atlantic on April 15, 1912. Violet was one of the few who survived the sinking.

The *Brittannic*- With the arrival of World War I the *Brittannic* was pressed into war service by the British government as a hospital ship. Along with the ship came none other than Violet Jessop, now a nurse. On November 21, 1916, the *Brittannic* struck a German mine while sailing in the Mediterranean. Violet was placed in a lifeboat which was lowered to the sea. But most of the lifeboats were drawn into one of the ship's propellers which was above the water due to the listing of the ship as it took on water. Twenty-eight deaths, the only ones recorded in the sinking, were due to the ship's propellers.

Violet and all on board her lifeboat dove overboard when their lifeboat was drawn toward the propeller's whirling blade.

She was sucked underwater and then surfaced beneath the capsized lifeboat just as it was smashed by the propeller. Violet, a non-swimmer, was whirled, beaten and battered under water only to surface behind the ship amid the remains of her less fortunate fellow passengers.

Violet Jessop survived all of her shipwrecks and continued sailing until her retirement in 1950 at the age of 63. She died (on land) in 1971. **Fight on!**

Reluctant Hero

INDIGNANTLY, 18 year old U.S. Army private, Jack Barkley, looked at his sergeant and said, "If you want to bump me off, for God's sake do it here!" It was October 7, 1918, and Pvt. Barkley had just been ordered out on a suicide mission behind German lines to observe enemy troop movement. After giving thought to the necessary logic of the mission, Pvt. Barkley relented, shook the sergeant's hand and said, "No hard feelings....but write a nice letter home to my folks." He then crawled out into the darkness beyond his lines.

As the day dawned, Pvt. Barkley saw German soldiers preparing to attack his fellow Americans. Unfortunately, his phone line had been cut, so he couldn't warn his regiment. Spying an abandoned French tank, Barkley stealthily retrieved an abandoned Maxim machine gun and several boxes of ammunition and slipped inside the tank. He positioned his gun to fire through the opening used by the French machine gun which had been removed. As 600 Germans poured from the woods on his left front, moving in front of him to the right, Barkley opened up. He raked the German troops with deadly fire killing scores, including many officers.

The Germans sent a 20 man patrol to take him out, but he shot down most of them and drove off the remainder. Then German artillery started raining shells down on his position. Barkley remembered an explosion and then blackness. When he woke up, he was bloodied and buried under ammunition boxes. He dug himself out, reset his machine gun and returned to blazing away at the Germans who had assumed him dead.

First he sprayed the artillery that had hit him. Free of that threat, he renewed his blistering attack on the German infantry. As a second German patrol peppered his tank with rifle fire and grenades, Barkley's water-cooled Maxim finally overheated and quit. He found a can of oil, poured it into the machine gun's water jacket and promptly dispatched his latest threat. Soon, the oil boiled away, filling the tank with acrid smoke. Then it quit again. Barkley felt that the end was near.

Suddenly, American artillery shells began to fall on the Germans and drove them back to the woods. While the enemy was held down by the artillery fire, Pvt. Barkley rolled out of his smoke filled tank and headed for his lines. Behind him he heard German artillery and turned to see it destroy his tank, but he was long gone. He had broken the German attack and saved unnumbered American lives. **Fight on!**

The LORD is on my side; I will not fear: what can man do unto me?

Psalm 118:6

O GOD the Lord, the strength of my salvation, thou hast covered my head in the day of battle.

Psalm 140:7

Servant of the Wrong Master

HIS god was Satan. He was his servant. On this balmy Australian April day in 1990, everyone would soon know what a loyal servant he was. He dressed in black and slung a bandolier of ammunition around his waist. He pulled the black balaclava over his face. He carved 666 into the back of his hands and then smeared the walls of his apartment with blood. Then he went hunting. He took a semi-automatic rifle and a pump shotgun to the balcony of his apartment. He looked down on the unsuspecting passers-by and thought of the death he was about to visit on them. He picked out an unsuspecting pedestrian, took careful aim and fired. His rifle barked...and no one fell. Again he fired. Again. Was the world suddenly bullet proof? No one he aimed at was hit. How was he to become Australia's most famous mass murderer if no one died? In Australia you have to kill more than four people at the same time to qualify as a mass murderer. But Rodney Dale was planning to greatly surpass that number.

Agitated, Dale went downstairs and out into the median strip of Australia's Gold Coast Highway. A car carrying an elderly couple approached and Dale hammered away at the driver and his wife. The wife was hit. The driver wasn't. Then he turned and fired more shots. No one fell wounded. Suddenly, of all things, a wedding procession approached. Dale took aim at the driver's head and shot him in the arm. He shot at the Bride and Groom through the car's back door and wounded a bridesmaid...in the leg. The next car was also met by a hail of Dale's bullets. Another arm wound. Another leg. Two women, one 72, the other 75, were now dead, well not <u>dead</u>, in Dale's sights. He blasted numerous rounds through their windshield, yet the women received only superficial wounds and didn't even bother stopping until they reached home. Dale continued flinging bullets at anyone he saw. Two men ran out of the first car Dale had shot at and tried to carry the wounded woman out of harm's way. Dale saw the two would-be heroes as his next two victims. He raised his rifle and sent a fusillade of bullets into the trunk, the doors and windows. But never hit one of the four people he aimed at.

By now 15 minutes had gone by and the police finally arrived. Sgt. Bob Baker, armed with only his .38 caliber service revolver, strode out and confronted Dale. From 50 feet away he called out, "If you don't put the gun down, I'll shoot you." Defiantly, Dale took aim at the lawman and opened fire time and time again....and never hit him once. Baker raised his pistol and fired. Dale dropped in a heap. He would live to go to prison. Australia's hopeful mass murderer and servant of Satan had fired 100 rounds at helpless, unarmed, unsuspecting civilians. When it was all over one person was dead and only seven were slightly wounded. **Who was the hero here?**

The Uncooperative Corpse

WHEN the freighter, *The Grandcamp* exploded at its mooring in Texas City, Texas, in 1947, longshoreman Joseph Vasquez was horribly injured. He was rushed to St. Joseph's Hospital, in very grave condition, where a doctor casually looked at the critically injured man and told a nurse, "Take him to 223, the morgue; he's gonna die." Vasquez was wheeled into a room full of dead bodies and covered with a sheet.

Hours later, a cleaning woman was startled half to death when one of the bodies in 223 asked if someone would please give him a drink of water. She reported this to the same doctor, who flatly stated, "Go ahead, give him all the water he wants. He's gonna die."

But Vasquez was an uncooperative corpse. His desire to live was greater than his injuries. After laying with the bodies for seven hours, doctors finally realized Vasquez wasn't quite ready to die. They removed him from the morgue, treated him and placed him in a regular hospital room. Joseph Vasquez survived. **Fight on!**

Save the Fleet!

IN late August, 1591, a small English naval force was in port on the island of Flores, in the Azores. Also in the area was a Spanish fleet. Both were spoiling for a fight. The small British fleet, under the command of Thomas Howard, consisted of only six men-of-war and six armed merchant vessels. The Spanish fleet, commanded by Don Alonzo de Bazan, boasted a total of fifty-three fighting ships.

On the morning of August 31, Howard got word that Bazan's fleet was sailing his way. In hopes of escape he quickly slipped his anchors and made for the open sea only to find fifteen heavily armed ships, the vanguard of Bazon's fleet, closing in on him. Broadsides were exchanged, then Howard broke for the open sea. His chances of out-distancing the Spanish fleet were slim. He knew that one-by-one his ships would be overrun and sunk or captured by the faster, more heavily armed Spaniards. There was no hope of survival.

Suddenly, Howard saw the 500 ton, 40 gun, English man-o-war, *Revenge*, under the command of Sir Richard Grenville, turn out of line and sail straight for the oncoming Spanish ships. Although hopelessly outgunned, Grenville was determined to buy time for the doomed British fleet to escape. With guns blazing like some "John Wayne of the Sea," Grenville sailed straight at the 60 gun, 1,500 ton *San Felipe.* The exchange of fire damaged *Revenge* but saw *San Felipe* limp away drawing water through her perforated hull. Next he attacked the *San Benardos* whose crew secured the *Revenge* with grappling hooks and attempted to board. Scores of Spanish boarders fell to the rabid Brits before the ships again parted. Next, Bazan's flagship, the *San Andrea,* mounted an attack that resulted in nothing more than its own sinking. Amazingly, an armed British merchant ship, the *George Noble,* sailed up beside the *Revenge* with an offer of assistance. Grenville would hear nothing of it as he ordered the *Noble's* captain to "save thyself, my friend, and leave me to my fate!" With that, the *George Noble* steered back for Howard's fleet.

Grenville's remarkable ship joined battle with as many as five Spanish galleons at one time, yet stayed afloat and in the battle. Several times the small British ship was grappled by two Spanish ships at once, yet the decimated British crew, only 150 strong before the carnage of battle, beat back every boarding attempt.

The sun set, but the battle continued to rage on through the night. Dawn found the gallant but battered English ship still afloat. She had sent three Spanish galleons to the bottom and saw another beach herself to escape the same fate. Severely wounded twice and dying, Grenville was powerless to stop his crew from surrendering their battered ship. But he had sunk three ships three times the size of his, put numerous others out of commission and depleted Spanish ranks by more than 2,000 men. He did all that, plus gave the British fleet time to escape to the open sea. **Fight on!**

The Slave With a Free Spirit

ELEVEN year old Olaudah Equiano, living in the African village of Ibo, thought nothing of the horrors of slavery. Raised well by loving parents, he and his five older brothers and one younger sister never pondered what the slaves their father owned had suffered. They never considered the terror they had experienced when they were surprised, captured and spirited away from parents, spouses, homes and happiness. Olaudah never thought about such horrors until the day in 1756 when it happened to him and his sister. That day, Islamic African slave traders stole into their village and whisked the two helpless children away before an alarm could be raised. Carried many miles away, they were separated and sold to different African masters. Olaudah's first master treated him well, almost like a son. But then he was sold, and sold again, and again, always moving in the direction of the Atlantic Ocean.

In spite of being a captive, Olaudah possessed a deep curiosity for all things new as well as an intellect that absorbed information. He quickly learned several languages during his travels. Once he reached the ocean he was swallowed into the bowels of a slave ship. The ship's white crewmen no more represented all white people than a black pimp represents all black people. But both deal in a form of slavery - one forbidden by the law, the other winked at by it.

While many slaves were sold in the Caribbean Islands, Olaudah was carried to Virginia colony and sold there to a lieutenant in the Royal Navy. He served shipboard for several years until he was sold to a Quaker in Philadelphia by the name of John King. King expanded Olaudah's education and in 1766, ten years after his abduction, allowed him to purchase his freedom. Olaudah then moved to England and continued his education.

Although he was now a young man, Olaudah never lost the spirit of curiosity he had as an 11 year old boy. At age 28, he assisted Dr. Charles Irving as he led an expedition into the Canadian Arctic in search of the Northwest Passage.

In 1785, now 40, he returned to Philadelphia where he married in 1792. He used his intellect and skills of oratory to lament the slave trade. Then, in 1797, the man who was always curious, who never stopped learning and who refused to allow his years as a slave to destroy his happiness, died. **Fight on!**

The Crazy Canadian

(*Author's Note:* On August 19, 1942, five thousand Sons of Canada landed at Dieppe, France. Before they had even landed, the element of surprise had been lost and the German defenders were ready for them. Nearly one thousand Canadians died trying to take their objective. Two thousand were able to withdraw to the boats. The remaining troops were taken prisoner.)

LIEUTENANT Colonel Charles Cecil Merritt, thirty-two, was the commander of the South Saskatchewan Regiment. His men had to cross a 550 foot long bridge to reach their objective. Mortars, machine gun and rifle fire drove the Canadians back. Then Lt. Col. Merritt arrived to appraise the situation. He announced, "Now men, we're going to get across. Follow me. Don't bunch up together, spread out. Here we go." Then he stood up and calmly strode out onto the bridge as though he was taking an afternoon stroll. As every German gun sent death his way, he turned back to his men and called out, "What's the matter with you fellows? You're not frightened are you? Come on over! There's nothing to worry about here."

How can you not follow such a man? He led a group across, then casually turned around and sauntered back to lead another group. Four times the seemingly bullet-proof colonel made the crossing until all his men were across.

Later he lead his men on an attack on a pillbox which he destroyed with a hand grenade. Although wounded twice, he continued to direct his men. A German sniper began to take his toll, so Lt. Col. Merritt hunted him down and killed him.

When the Canadians were ordered to evacuate, he fought

his men back to the beach, saw them onto landing craft and then announced he would stay behind to hold off the Germans while the others made their escape.

Lt. Col. Merritt had fought for six hours. He was taken prisoner along with almost two thousand others. He later escaped and was recaptured and was finally released in April of 1945, when American forces overran his prison camp. **Fight on!**

Breaking INTO Auschwitz

DURING World War II several hundred thousand Jews were sent to the Nazi death camp known as Auschwitz. Hundreds of thousands died. Some survived. A few even escaped. But only one man ever tried and succeeded to break into Auschwitz.

His name is Witold Pilecki. He was a member of the Secret Polish Army, a resistance group dedicated to fighting Nazi oppression. Pilecki intentionally got himself arrested under the assumed name of a man who had failed to report for duty with the German Army. This merited him a stay in Auschwitz. Why did Pilecki want inside a Nazi death camp? His mission was to found a resistance movement within the camp itself, as well as smuggle reports of what was going on in the camp to the outside world.

Within three months of his arrest in September of 1940, he had already founded five resistance groups. By the spring of 1941, ten more were in place. While in the hospital with pneumonia he contracted while being force to stand naked outside for hours in February, he organized a cell within the hospital. He soon had over 500 men working for him.

By early in 1943 his position became unsafe. The Gestapo was on his trail They would soon identify, collar and kill him. So, he simply left! He got himself added to a work party that went outside of the camp. He slipped off his striped prison uniform, revealing civilian clothes beneath, and at an opportune time slipped away. He then made his way to Warsaw to report on his assignment. **Fight on!**

Brave Leap for Life

AS Wesley Autrey waited for his train in the New York subway in January, 2007, a nineteen year old young man encountered a problem and fell down onto the tracks as a train came rushing toward him. Autrey reached down and tried to pull the young man back up to the platform but couldn't. With no time to lose he made a split-second decision and dove down top of him. Thrusting him between the rails he covered him with his body as the train rolled over them. Neither was injured. The young man was taken to the hospital to be evaluated. Autrey refused treatment and went on his way. **Fight on!**

Pushing Himself Beyond His Fear

As a young boy, Australian Ian Boughton had watched helplessly as his youngest brother drowned. It instilled an unnatural terror for water into him.

When Boughton was fully grown and a Senior Constable at the Newcastle branch of Police Rescue he took a call in April of 1995 that would revive every horrible thought that his fear of water would yield.

Stephen Lamb, a commercial diver, had gone down into a water-filled chamber that morning. The BHP iron works cooled its steel making operation with water drawn from the nearby Hunter River. A pump draws water through six filters into six chambers. Suspended about a foot and a half from the floor in the middle of each chamber a pipe about two feet in diameter rises vertically for six feet and then turns 90 degrees to feed water directly into a high volume pump.

The filters for chamber #5 had been removed for cleaning and Lamb was doing an inspection of the seal before the filters were reinstalled. For Lamb's safety, #5 pump had to be shut off. No one ever established exactly why, but it wasn't. While Lamb was in the chamber, the pump cycled on. The resulting suction swept him off his feet and up into the pipe. In the process, he lost the airline from the surface that provided compressed air to breath.

Topside, his assistants felt Lamb's airline unwind rapidly and realized what must have happened. While one man yanked vainly on the line, the other ran and called for the operator to shut down the pump. A diver entered the chamber and found Lamb's airline leading up into the pipe. Hoping to free Lamb, he tugged on the line only to have Lamb's harness and regulator pull free. Stephen Lamb was pinned up in the access pipe with no way to reach him.

When Constable Boughton arrived, he realized there was no time to waste. There was a chance Lamb was trapped in an air pocket. Boughton was not a strong swimmer, was claustrophobic and afraid of water. But he did what had to be done. He told the other divers, "How about you put this gear on me and teach me how to use it while you are strapping it on." Then he descended into the silt-darkened waters, found the pipe opening and pondered what to do. He sat on the chamber floor, stuck one arm above him and one behind and forced himself up into the tight confines of the intake pipe. Up he wiggled in crushing claustrophobic darkness. Finally, he came to the elbow. In blackness he forced his body around the 90 degree bend. Stretching out in the terrible darkness, he inched forward until his fingers discovered Stephen Lamb's hand. He pulled on Lamb's hand but he didn't move. His foot was jammed inside the pump. Again he pulled. Nothing. Over and over he yanked on the trapped man until he finally pulled him loose. Slowly he inched backward to the elbow. By super human determination he wrestled the man around the bend, down the shaft and up to the surface. After 25 minutes work, paramedics got Lamb's heart restarted and he was rushed to a nearby hospital. Unfortunately, he did not recover.

Ian Boughton had overcome his most deep-seated fears to help someone who needed help. **Fight on!**

Six Desperate Men

ON September 12, 1874, during an Indian War, six men of the 6th U.S. Cavalry were assigned to carry a dispatch back to their main supply camp. The 6th Cavalry was deep in Indian territory in western Texas.

Once out on the plains the men were set upon by a force of about one hundred twenty-five Indians. They rode hard for a ravine, dismounted and took up positions. Private George W. Smith, who was guarding the horses, was shot through the arm as twenty-five Indians charged him. The other five gathered the horses while Smith struggled to safety.

Finding their position untenable, they executed a fighting withdrawal as fire came from all directions. All day long they fought from one location to another while the Indians made repeated charges.

Finally as they were making for a knoll where a buffalo wallow was located two of them were wounded but still made it to the wallow. Pvt. Smith was also hit again and fell quite a distance from safety. Although the troopers thought him to be dead, he was seen to move. At that point Scout Amos Chapman announced, "Now boys, keep those infernal redskins off me and I will run down and pick up Smith and bring him back before they can get at me." Armed with a pistol Chapman dashed to the wounded man, lifted him on his back and started back. When he had gone about 30 yards, fifteen Indians on horseback tried to cut between him and safety. They were Indians that knew him because he had helped them in the past. As they charged him they cried, "Amos! Amos! We have got you now." Chapman dropped Smith and opened up with his pistol as his comrades also lit into them. They scattered, so Chapman hoisted Smith back up and started running.

Another band attacked. An Indian that Chapman had personally given food to many times, shot him. The bullet shattered his leg just above the ankle. He never wavered. He kept running on the end of the broken bone, dragging his foot behind him.

The men, low on ammunition, fought on until dark, accounting for twenty Indians killed and numerous others wounded. That was too much for the Indians, and they stole off during the night not to return.

The next morning Smith died and Chapman and the two other wounded troopers were too bad to move. The men were forced to drink the vile water in the wallow that was polluted with their own blood. They kept vigil all day long watching for resumed attacks. They never came. That night a relief column found them and took them to the supply camp.

All six received the Medal of Honor. **Fight on!**

A Son's Love

Billy Corcoran was nine years old that cold winter's day in 1994 in Victoria, Australia, when his love for his father was put to the test.

Greg Corcoran, a farmer, was in a cattle pen when a Hereford bull turned on him and drove his head into the man's chest. Corcoran flew through the air and landed hard, damaging his spine and leaving him paralyzed from the waist down. Billy heard his father cry out and then saw him lying on the ground with the bull about to attack him again. He leaped into the pen armed with only a stick, and stood, like a tiny human wall, between the bull and his father. When the bull moved in, the boy wailed on its face with the stick until it broke. The beast turned away, and Billy threw his dad a second stick for defense, then jumped the rail again to open the gate and let the bull out of the pen. Suddenly the animal doubled back and headed for the helpless man. Billy jumped back into the pen, grabbed the stick from his dad and resumed his assault on the animal. That stick broke also. As the angry bull pawed the ground, Billy raced forward and kicked it in the nose, yelling and waving his jacket. The bull turned and shot through the gate.

Next, the noble nine year old ran to his father's car and called for an ambulance. Then he drove the car and parked it so as to shield his dad from the frigid winter's wind. He grabbed a blanket, covered him and climbed in next to him.

Greg was rushed to the hospital. In a few days Greg's mobility returned and he recovered completely, never to doubt his son's love. **Fight on!**

"I love Dad and I didn't want him to get hurt. Dad was just laying there; he couldn't do nothing. I had to do something. I couldn't just sit there and watch."

Billy

Permission Granted!

BY 1987 twenty-six year old David Moody (not his real name), had been a missionary in Papua New Guinea a year. One morning he was out giving away Bibles outside of Port Moresby. After stopping at a store to buy some water and pass out gospel leaflets, he returned to his truck for more and found himself facing five sinister men They demanded money; he told them he had none, that he was a missionary. "Sorry" they said, and walked away. David locked his truck, turned around and caught a 2"x4" in the ribs. The blow was so great it broke three ribs and knocked him out. While unconscious, the men kicked him in the face, damaging his left eye. Then they cut his face and neck 40 times.

When he came to, the leader, a renegade soldier demanded, "I want your money! I want your truck keys!" David put out an urgent prayer, "God, what am I supposed to do? Can I hit him?" The answer came back, "Yes."

The five men stood menacingly and laughed as David stumbled to his feet. He turned and acted like he was getting his wallet. The Big Man dropped the 2"x4" and stepped forward to get the wallet. David came around and hit the man with everything he had. His punch broke the Big Man's jaw, knocking him out, breaking three of his own fingers. The other men picked up the 2'x4'. David then pulled his knife and defiantly faced them. They backed down and dragged the Big Man away. Young David reached out and put a Gospel tract in the Big Man's pocket. Both the Big Man and his wife later came to Christ. **Fight on!**

He Chickened Out

IN the days before modern four-lane interstate highways, there was what we would call a little "Ma & Pa" motel/gas station/restaurant on a two-lane highway in rural Kentucky. The proprietor was nearing 65 years old and looked to the sale of his successful little motel and restaurant to secure his financial stability in retirement. Then came the bombshell. The government was going to build Interstate I-75 just a few miles west of his restaurant. Traffic from his small two-lane road would be diverted by the modern four-lane. Overnight the value of his business plummeted. Bankruptcy and poverty loomed on the horizon.

But the bubbly old gentleman wasn't one to cry, "Foul" or give in to hopelessness. He had been a soldier, ferryboat captain, insurance salesman, railroad laborer, service station operator, inn keeper and had even run for U.S. Senate in 1951. So, he surveyed his customers to see what they thought was his restaurant's best dish. That done, at age 65 and with only $105 in his pocket, he loaded up his car with buckets of what is now a world famous product and Col. Harlin Sanders (1890 - 1980) ventured out and began the worldwide chain of restaurants we now know as Kentucky Fried Chicken. How did he get paid? He told his managers, "Just pay me out of the profits when you get some money." He died a millionaire. **Fight on!**

(*Author's Note:* Founded in 1956, by 1964 there were 800 Kentucky Fried Chicken stores in the United States. By 2006 there were over 10,000 stores in fifty-four countries. Take exit #29 off I-75 and you can still enjoy the Colonel's famous chicken at the original "Sander's Court Motel.")

Only a Hundred and Thirty-Two

ON October 8, 1918, a patrol of American soldiers was sent behind German lines to locate and silence several machine gun nests that were raking American lines. The sixteen man patrol captured a German major and his staff while they were eating their breakfast. Suddenly, nearby German soldiers opened up on the Americans, killing six and wounding three others. While the remaining doughboys covered their German prisoners, Corporal (later Sergeant) Alvin York, crawled forward and waged a devastating one-man war on the enemy.

Due to his Tennessee hills upbringing, York could hit a squirrel a football field away so he had no trouble "plinking" German machine gunners one by one. Finally, a six man squad made a bayonet charge against the wily Tennessean. Starting at the last man, York dropped each one until his Enfield was empty and only the lead officer was left. With the German just a few feet away, York raised his .45 and ended the charge. Then he reloaded his rifle and renewed his devastating fire.

The captured German officer had had enough. He told York he would surrender his men if York would just stop killing them. OK. The German blew a whistle and shouted orders, and Cpl. York and his men gathered up the startled, but relieved, German prisoners and marched them back to the American lines.

Later, the brigadier general at the headquarters remarked to York, "I hear you've captured the whole d-----d German Army." The Tennessee Christian responded humbly, "No, sir, I only have a hundred and thirty-two." **Fight on!**

It Was Their Ship!

THE fire and explosions that ravaged the *USS Forrestal* on July 29, 1967, resulted in many sailors being blown off, or being forced to jump off, the burning ship. Others, still onboard, received horrendous burns and blast related injuries. As soon as helicopters were able, to they shuttled injured sailors to the sick bay of the nearby *USS Oriskany*. Many men who had been plucked from the water were also off-loaded there. Inevitably, this resulted in some men who had gone overboard from the Forrestal, being deposited on the Oriskany, who had received no real injuries other than a sound dunking.

As the *Oriskany's* medical administration officer made his rounds through the injured *Forrestal* sailors aboard his ship, he came upon two sailors from the *Forrestal* who had received no serious injuries. Blown off the ship, covered in jet fuel and having gulped huge amounts of seawater before being picked up, the two were now frantic. As the officer approached them the men blurted out, "We've got to get back to our ship! Our ship's on fire! We've got to go back to our ship!"

Appreciating their sense of duty but not willing to return the men to an uncertain fate on the burning *Forrestal*, he told them, "You don't need to go anywhere. They have enough people to take care of themselves. Just stay here." Minutes later he returned to find the men gone. They had caught a helicopter back to the *Forrestal* to lend their help. After all, it was their ship. **Fight on!**

Sailors Who Never Faltered

THE *USS Forrestal*, like all aircraft carriers, was steered by two massive rudders. These were mounted to two huge shafts that penetrate the bottom of the hull and proceed up into the ship, one on the port (left) side, and one on the starboard (right) side. These giant shafts each pass through a room that is eight feet by eight feet square, two decks in height and constantly manned by three sailors. Although the rudders are controlled remotely from the bridge, the three men are stationed there as a precaution. If steering control from the bridge is lost due to battle damage, these sailors can turn the rudders manually. Or, if one steerage compartment is battle-damaged, the sailors manning it can transfer steering control to the other steerage compartment across the ship from them.

When the fire began on the port aft section of the *Forrestal's* flight deck, Seaman James L. Blaskis, Kenneth L. Fasth and Ronald R. Ogrinc, manning the port steerage compartment far below, were too isolated to be endangered or even aware of the problem. But when the first of nine 1,000 lb. bombs exploded, things changed quickly. Shrapnel from the huge bomb blew straight down through the ship and into their compartment. Instantly the three men were seriously injured and, in just minutes, cut off and surrounded by flames. They had no way of escape and, above them, bomb after bomb sent white hot shrapnel down through their station as streams of burning jet fuel also poured down around them.

Twenty-one year old Seaman Blaskis, who was in charge

of the group, administered first aid to his two wounded fellow sailors and called the bridge with a plea for help. But the men were cut off, and no help could possibly reach them. Meanwhile, the fires kept closing in on them.

Forty-eight year old Chief Engineeer, Merv Rowland, was directing fire fighting crews. After several well-meaning sailors had lied to Blakis, assuring him that help would soon arrive, Rowland got on the inter-ship phone. With the firmness that only his many years in service could muster, and the love only a father could feel, he explained that no help would be reaching the young men. After a long silence Blaskis quietly replied, "...Sir, we're dying." Yes, they were.

"Just hang in there, son...I don't think there's anything I can do for you."

"Yes sir."

As the fire raged, there was a very real possibility that steering control could be lost, greatly hampering the fire-fighting efforts. The *Forrestal* had destroyers on either side, just yards away, with hoses trained on the carrier's fires. A loss of steering control would endanger them. As tough as it was, Rowland called Blaskis and gave the three dying sailors their last orders. They had to transfer control of the port rudder to the starboard steerage control room. The dying sailors dutifully carried out the order in spite of their horrible wounds. Then, one by one, Rowland listened as they died.

Of these three it has been said, "They were sailors to the end. They never begged for mercy. They never whined. They never whimpered." **They fought on!**

We All Appreciate Johnnie Frye's Friend

JOHNNIE Frye was one of the very first Pony Express riders. As he would gallop along one part of his seventy-five mile portion of the trip from St. Joseph, Missouri, to San Francisco, California, a young woman on horseback would dash out to meet him, pull up alongside and pass over cakes and cookies. But she saw that Frye had trouble managing the cookies with one hand, his other occupied with the reins of his galloping horse.

One day the young lady galloped out and caught up with Frye. She planted a round cake with a hole in the middle on Frye's finger which he easily handled. The donut had been born. **Enjoy!**

No Bluffing in Bluffton

A hope-to-be carjacker rapped on the window of a man's car in Bluffton, South Carolina, demanding the man surrender his car. Not being well trained in how to be a good victim, the man decided to fight back instead. First he slammed the car door open right into his assailant's legs. Then he threw his hot coffee in his face. Then he jumped on him. The startled, injured and terrified criminal managed to stagger to his feet and was last seen running away in stark terror. **Fight on!**

One Last Brave Act

On August 5, 1944, just over 1,100 Japanese POW's in the Cowra POW camp 227 miles west of Sydney, Australia, launched a mad suicidal breakout. The prisoners, ashamed of having been captured, planned to storm the fences, attack a small army training camp nearby, gain weapons and head into the countryside. (The town of Cowra was 1 ½ miles away.)

At the given signal, armed with hundreds of knives, forks, baseball bats and other improvised weapons, they attacked. Their first objective was a lone, unmanned, machine gun, which they planned to turn on their Australian guards.

Recognizing the prisoners goal, two Aussie privates raced for the machine gun and opened fire. Scores were killed, but the swarming mass of screaming Japanese simply stormed right over the bodies of their comrades. Realizing they couldn't stay where they were, Pvt. Ben Hardy told Pvt. Ralph Jones to run for it. But then, rather than seek escape himself, he dutifully removed and hid the breach block, rendering the weapon useless. Both Jones and Hardy were overrun and stabbed, kicked and clubbed to death. However with the gun being useless; the escape was doomed.

Many fanatical prisoners stabbed themselves to death or slit the throats of wounded comrades.

Over 200 Japanese died, quelling the uprising. But we will never know how many innocent lives were saved by the last brave act of two Aussie soldiers. **Fight on!**

Victory Without A Weapon

SEVENTY miles off Key West, Florida is Dry Tortuga (Turtle) Island. In the mid-19th Century the United States built Fort Thomas Jefferson on the small island to control shipping in the Gulf of Mexico. When Union Major L. G. Arnold arrived with 66 artillerymen on January 19, 1861, the fort, as yet, had no cannon mounted. As they worked on the first gun mount, an armed ship dropped anchor and a small boat came ashore. A courier from the ship demanded the surrender of the fort to the State of Florida. Without a gun they had no hope of winning a battle with an armed ship. But Major Arnold wasn't so quick to give up. After he read the demand for surrender he rushed to the gunport and called down to the Southern sailor, "Tell your captain I will blow his ship out of the water if he's not gone in ten minutes!" The messenger returned to his ship which weighed anchor and fled. **Bluff on!**

An Aggressive Defense

JIM Mariotte's friend had shot a moose out on the Alaska tundra. They had loaded up his friend and his wife with meat and the two had headed for camp soon to be followed by Jim, who planned to finish skinning the animal's head so his friend could mount it.

Several times Jim heard something in the nearby bushes. "A bird," he thought. Then a terrifying chill went through him as he suddenly realized there were no birds around anywhere. Before he could react to this realization, the noise was behind him. He turned to see a grizzly bear step out of the bushes so close he could have touched it. The bear looked at the man, turned and ran back into the bushes, but a second later turned back around and attacked. In savage fury, the beast grabbed Mariotte by the right thigh and shook the 225 lb. man like a rag doll and tossed him, as it continued running. Jim landed on his back, head down in a slight hollow in the tundra. Then the bear doubled back to examine the moose carcass.

Mariotte laid as still as death. Like so many, he had heard that if you played dead, a bear might leave you alone. Remarkably, he still had his short-bladed skinning knife in his left hand.

The bear looked at the moose. Then it looked at Mariotte. Then, as though it had reached a decision, the beast again charged the injured hunter, clamping its massive jaws down on his right knee. Mariotte forgot all about playing dead and in a fit of rage, he drove his small knife into the animal's neck repeatedly. The bear reacted to the counterattack by letting go of

Mariotte and pulled back about 60 feet. As the bear hesitated, Mariotte got to his feet. Then the bear attacked him for the third time. The bear clamped its jaws into his left thigh and threw him back into the depression, but Mariotte fought back gamely, stabbing the beast over and over again in the neck. Mariotte's efforts were having an effect, for the bear snapped at the knife. But as he savaged Mariotte's hand he also drove the knife into his own tongue and lower jaw with each bite.

Again the disoriented animal backed off, not sure what to make of the situation. Mariotte rose to his full 6 foot 7 inch height as the bear charged, this time burying its teeth into Mariotte's lower leg. Then Mariotte bent down and slammed the knife again into the bear's neck. But when he pulled his hand back up, he had somehow lost hold of the knife and it was now buried somewhere in the animal's neck. Undaunted, he bent down, grabbed the grizzly's fur with his right hand and searched for the handle of the knife with the left. He had every intention of killing his assailant on the spot.

For the first time perhaps, the bear sensed the tide-of-battle had shifted and that it was losing. It unlocked its jaws, tore free of Mariotte's grip and dashed about 50 feet away, this time it was facing away from his intended victim.

Again, breaking the rules of the "experts," Mariotte bolted away down the trail toward his two friends. When he looked back, the grizzly was standing on its hind legs watching him. But it did not pursue him. It had had enough.

On the trail, Mariotte met his hunting partner who had dropped his pack and backtracked when he heard the sounds of the attack. His friends helped him back to camp and dressed his wounds as best they could. But this big man's fight wasn't over yet. A September blizzard set upon the trio and kept them pinned down for three days. Finally it broke, and Mariotte was flown out by a bush pilot to the hospital in Fairbanks.

Jim recovered and was right back out on the tundra a year later. **Fight on!**

"I Did Not Tell Them"

AS the Japanese battled to retain the island of Guadalcanal during World War II, they demanded that the natives assist them by giving them information on American troop positions. One such unfortunate villager was Vouza, a retired Sergeant-major in the local police force. The Japanese demanded information about the Americans from him. He refused to tell them anything. They then tied him to a tree and drove a bayonet into his body. Then they demanded their answers. He said nothing. Again, a Japanese soldier drove his bayonet into the helpless man. Again they stood by the writhing man and waited. Nothing. Five times they stabbed the brave man. Five times he withstood them and then slumped in his bonds. Assured of his imminent death, his cruel tormentors turned and walked away.

Sometime later the grievously wounded man came to. Seeing he was alone, he managed to chew through his bonds and make his way to the American hospital in the town of Lunga. His last words before he lost consciousness were, "I did not tell them."

Vouza survived and was awarded the British George Medal for bravery. **Hold out!**

He Failed

HE had an idea. He gave it a try. It didn't work. It was a great idea so he tried again. He failed again. He thought of another way to do it. It flopped. He tried it another way. He failed...and failed...and failed..and failed...and failed several **hundred times**. And then, on October 21, 1879, Thomas Alva Edison got his electric light to work. Aren't you glad he didn't quit!? **Fight on!**

(*Author's Note:* Thomas Edison got his first patent June 1, 1879. Between that date and 1910 he was awarded 1,093 patents. He averaged one patent every 11 days between 1879 and 1910.)

"Dear companions, every hope has vanished for us too. The black damp is stronger than before. It is best we retreat to where we were before and wait for death."

Walter Waite, a survivor

"Dear brothers, at this point there is nothing for us to hope for as far as leaving this tomb alive. We might as well resign ourselves to die as men. Hold dear those few lines you wrote. Before we die, however, my idea is to pray to God not to give us such a cruel death."

Walter Waite

"In the day when I cried thou answeredst me, and strengthenedst me with strength in my soul."

Psalm 138:3

"Companions, I've got another idea..."

Walter Waite

"I've Got Another Idea..."

(*Author's Note:* The coal mine in Cherry, Illinois, was opened in 1905 and heralded as the safest in the country. It was declared fireproof. On November 12, 1909, it caught fire. Two hundred and fifty-nine miners lost their lives. The fire burned so fiercely that it was March of 1910 before it was finally extinguished and all the bodies recovered.)

TWO hundred and seventy-nine miners were trapped over three hundred feet underground when the Cherry Mine fire cut them off from the hoisting shaft. Two hundred fifty-nine of them died. The other twenty tried to. This group of castaways from various locations in the mine was led by Walter Waite, an assistant mine manager who had chosen to stay behind and try to rescue miners rather than escape when it was still possible. The men retreated deeper into the mine in hopes of escaping the fire, but the mine was filling with "black damp" an odorless gas that could fell a man in seconds and kill him in a minute.

For three days, twenty-one survivors had wandered around trying to find a way out, always being cut off by flames and smoke. On November 14, one of the men took a few steps and dropped. He was dead. Black damp. Without food and water and with the mine corridors silently filling with black damp, the men knew they too would soon be dead. They wrote letters to their families, prayed, sang *"Abide With Me"* and listened to a sermon by William Clelland, one of the miners. Then they sang *"Nearer My God To Thee"* and at 9 PM laid down and patiently waited for the gas to put them to sleep.

An hour later Walter Waite called out, "Companions, I've got another idea and it's this. Do you all believe that if we make two walls, one at the entry of the road, we can hold back the black damp from us for a couple of days? And if you believe it's opportune to do this job, it's better to start working at once." The wall held death back for five more days. Then on November 20 they decided to try again for the hoisting shaft. They broke a hole in their makeshift wall and seven of the strongest set out...and ran into a group of rescuers who were fighting the fire while recovering bodies. They never expected to find anyone alive.

Twenty men decided to give up and die, but then lived because one chose to **Fight on!**

They Tried to Go Over Him

NO man who saw it happen lived to tell about it. The rage. The violence. The desperation. It all happened as August 7, 1942, became August 8 of 1942. The place was the small island of Tulagi in the Solomon Island chain in the South Pacific. The Marines had landed and established a tenuous beachhead and then prepared for the inevitable Japanese counterattack. That night they hit the line with four separate assaults. The center of the line was the weakest. A breakthrough there would allow the Japanese to attack Marine Headquarters as well as roll up the line. That's where Marine Private 1st Class John Ahrens was positioned. That's where they found him the next morning, with blood oozing from two bullet wounds to the chest and three bayonet wounds to his body. Around his foxhole lay the bodies of thirteen Imperial Japanese soldiers. Beside him lay the body of a dead Japanese sergeant. Draped across his legs was a dead Japanese officer. As Captain Lewis Walt attended the dying marine, Ahrens gasped, "Captain, they tried to come over me last night, but I don't think they made it." They hadn't. Private Johnny Ahrens had paid the ultimate price of valor. **Fight on!**

Two Heroes at Once

AMERICANS are a heroic people. They never turn away from overwhelming odds and never fail, even in the midst of disasters, to think about the safety of "the other guy." And among this race of courageous people there are certain groups that excel at acts of both bravery and compassion. Policemen, firemen and members of the U.S. military are among those groups. When Muslim terrorists attacked the twin towers of the World Trade Center on September 11, 2001, members of the two former groups shined like beacons of courage and selflessness.

After the South Tower collapsed, firemen knew its sister, the North Tower, was also doomed. Orders were given to abandon efforts to fight the fire on the 86th floor and to evacuate the building.

Josephine Harris had started down the stairs with the others from her office on the 73rd floor, but at fifty-nine years old, the going was slow. By the time she reached the 14th floor, she was completely exhausted and unable to move another step. As she gasped for air, a group of six firemen from Ladder 6 and a police officer came rushing down from the 27th floor. They stopped. The building was in eminent danger of collapsing and these men all wanted to get out. However, no one was about to leave this exhausted grandmother behind. David Lim, the policeman, and Bill Butler, a fireman, supported Josephine between them and started down. But hesitating to help Josephine had stolen crucial time; they would not make it out of the building before it fell. As everything around them gave way, neither Lim nor Butler, faced with certain death, thought of themselves. Instead, both thought of Josephine and both threw themselves on top of the helpless lady in an effort to protect her. The stairs beneath them fell away and the 110 story building collapsed around them.

As the dust settled, the leader of the team, Captain Jay Jonas, was amazed to find that, not only was he alive, but all the men with him were. And so was their unsteady charge, Josephine Harris.

Firefighters found Jonas and his crew and pulled them from the wreckage. Later, Jonas would sum up their survival by saying, "We all thought Josephine was walking much too slow. But in reality she was the one with the perfect timing. God gave us the courage to help her, and that's how we ourselves were saved." **Fight on!**

He Went Down With His Ship

IN 1854 the oceangoing side-wheeler, *Arctic*, was the *Queen Mary* of her day. She crossed the Atlantic between New York and Liverpool in record time carrying the social elite.

On Sept. 27, 1854, while returning to the U.S. she collided with the French steamship, *Vesta*, which survived the accident. The *Arctic* sunk in five hours. Of the 408 people on board, only eighty-seven survived. Only twenty-two of this number were passengers, all male; not a woman or child survived. This was because most of the crewmen deserted, manned the lifeboats and left the rest to their fate.

The ship's captain, James C. Luce, was not among these deserters. For five hours he fought to save his ship and its passengers. When he gave the order to abandon ship he ordered, "Women and children first." The panicked crewmen ignored his order and took to the boats and left. He physically wrestled with crewmen in an effort to make them let the passengers board the lifeboats. Once the boats were away he went about handing life preservers to those on board. When he had done all he could, he went to his quarters where his crippled 11 year old son, Willie, and his attendant waited. The servant tried to give the captain his own life preserver but the captain refused it. Then he carried Willie to the top of the paddle box that shrouded the huge 35 foot paddle wheels.

The ship slid stern first at a slight angle beneath the waves. Luce and Willie were sucked down with the suction of the sinking ship. The swirling water separated the two as they struggled for the surface. Luce broke the surface and was pulled under again. When he resurfaced, he started towards his son when suddenly one of the paddle wheel boxes, having torn loose from the ship, shot out of the water like a huge fish and crashed down on them. Luce received a gash on the head, Willie was killed. But the wheel box floated inverted like a small boat. Captain Luce made his way to it. Once inside he began plucking people from the water, men, women and children, determined to save some of his passengers. Eventually there were twelve aboard. But the crashing waves and cold Atlantic water claimed them one-by-one. Only Luce and two other men remained when they were picked up two days later by a passing ship.

Captain James Luce, known to all as a gentleman, had done his duty, saved all he could and then gone down with his ship. But he survived. He died July 9, 1879, at age seventy-four. **Do right!**

"He was American, he was a soldier, he was a brother and he was one of us. And there was nothing gonna stop us from doing what we knew we had to do and we knew we did right."

Staff Sgt. Dan Brown, who removed the RPG round from Pvt. Moss

Army Strong

ON March 16, 2006, n Army convoy was ambushed in Paktika Province in Afghanistan. A rocket-powered grenade (RPG) slammed through the door of an up-armored HUMVEE without exploding and lodged inside Pvt. Channing Moss. The round shattered Moss' pelvis and literally stretched from one side of the soldier to the other. A MEDEVAC helicopter was called for. Army regulations forbid transporting a soldier with unexploded ordinance in them due to the potential for catastrophic loss to the ship, its crew and the other wounded, but chopper pilot CW2 Jorge Correa and his crew chose to transport the wounded soldier anyway. Upon arrival at the Army medical facility surgeons and staff volunteered to try the save Moss, whose heart stopped during the process. A bomb disposal officer helped remove the grenade, took it to a safe location and detonated it.

Not expected to live, and then never expected to walk, Pvt. Moss underwent four major surgeries and later stood and walked to receive his Purple Heart. He said, "I wanted to walk and get my medal. I wanted to stand up, to let them know I fought hard to get where I came from. They say, 'Army Strong,' I wanted to be an example of that, and I was. So I stood up, I walked over and got my medal." **Fight on!**

The New York Tea Party

IN late August, 1776, British Gen. Howe's Redcoats had quickly taken Long Island from the Continental Army. In a Divinely assisted retreat across the East River to New York from Brooklyn, Gen. George Washington saved his 9,000 man army. But it was still in peril. New York was on a long finger of land; all the British general had to do was march his troops behind Washington and he and the Colonial Army would cease to exist. Seeing this, Washington moved his troops north, out of the trap, leaving 1,500 men under Israel Putnam to cover the retreat.

The British landed at Kips Bay. They planned to cross the peninsula, cut Putnam off and take 1,500 men out of the Colonial cause. Enter Mrs. Robert Murray, a Quaker mother of twelve in her 50's. She met Gen. Howe and convinced him and his generals to come to her house for tea. There, for more than two hours she fed them and kept them occupied. By the time the British officers had finished their meal Putnam and his troops had escaped. **Fight on!**

A Determined Young Survivor

IN March of 1851 Rayse Oatman, his wife, Mary Ann, and their seven children, ages 1 - 17 years old, were slowly traversing the desolate prairie of Arizona Territory toward Fort Yuma on their way to California. While in camp, the pioneer family was approached by a group of Yavapai Indians. They courteously fed the group, gave them some gifts and talked. Without warning, the Indian leader let out a signal cry and the group fell on the surprised, defenseless family with knives and war clubs. All but three of the family were killed and their belongings stolen.

Two girls, Olive, 15, and Mary Ann, 7, were kept and later sold to another tribe. Mary Ann died from the hardship while, after five long years of captivity, Olive was recovered by whites.

Fourteen year old Lorenzo was clubbed several times in the head and then tossed 60 feet down the hillside. He lay there stunned and bleeding, listening to the dying cries of his family. Lorenzo awoke the next day, dizzy, nauseous and badly battered. His body didn't want to obey his commands. The option to lay there and die attractively presented itself. Then the resolute 14 year old said to himself, "I will get up. I will walk, or, if not, I will spend the last remnant of my shattered strength to crawl out of this place." He crawled until he could walk. Then he walked until he stumbled upon another group of settlers who nursed him back to health. He finally made it to California and was eventually reunited with his rescued sister. **Fight on!**

Out You Go

DURING the battle of Montrebeau Woods, during World War I, Corporal Harold W. Roberts was piloting his lumbering tank across an artillery-created moonscape. Suddenly, the tank nosed into a ten foot deep shell crater that had been filled with water by the recent rains. Far from being watertight, the tank began to fill with water in seconds, so fast, in fact, that Roberts knew there would only be time enough for either him or the tank's other crewman to escape. Cpl. Roberts said to his gunner rather matter-of-factly, "Well, only one of us can get out, so out you go." And with that he grabbed the man and stuffed him up and out the hatch...and then promptly drowned. **Fight on!**

Not Settling for Safety

WORLD War II was looming on the horizon when James left a successful career and tried enlisting in the Army in March of 1941, nine months before Pearl Harbor. The tall, thin, handsome 33 year old was rejected for being ten pounds underweight. He appealed the decision and was accepted. Because he was a pilot, he was assigned to be a flight instructor, a nice, fairly safe job away from combat. Nope! James wouldn't have it, so he volunteered for combat duty and was assigned to the Eighth Air Force in England. From there he flew bombing missions aboard B-24's. Later he was promoted up through the ranks, finishing World War II as a colonel.

With the war finally over, he returned to his old job as Jimmy Stewart, the movie star. **Fight on!**

Sometimes You've Just Got to Laugh

DURING the closing days of the Civil War, a cornfield separated two units of United States and Confederate armies. Both sides had, by their non-aggressive actions, agreed to a de facto cease-fire. One day groups from the opposing sides encountered each other in a cornfield while gathering provisions. The men eyed each other but, without malice, continued to gather the desperately needed corn for their starving comrades.

Suddenly they spooked a wild hog and both sides took off after the mobile pork chop machine. In the excitement one Rebel fired at the beast barely missing a Union pursuers. Suddenly, guns were at the ready as a wary U.S. trooper queried, "Halloo, there, Johnny! What do you mean by that?"

The offending Rebel, somewhat chagrined, hollered back, "I'm not shooting at you, but at that other hog."

The war was momentarily put on hold while men from both sides lost themselves in laughter. **Laugh a little!**

Home Run!

SEVENTY-FOUR year old John Magred and his wife were tending their little store in rural New Hampshire in January, 2007, when two young men entered and demanded their money. Rather than surrender to his much younger adversaries, Magred reached under the counter where he kept a baseball bat and literally came up swinging. The two would-be robbers fled. Magred kept his money. **Fight on!**

Alone in Antarctica

IN November of 1922, twenty-nine year old Douglas Mawson was part of a three man team from a large expedition to Antarctica whose goal was to chart almost two thousand miles of unexplored coastline. For five weeks they battled the brutal Antarctic weather and faithfully recorded coastal features. Following a vicious blizzard, the men put most of their food on one sledge to which was harnessed their strongest dog team. Lt. Belgrave Ninnis of the British Army scouted ahead on skis for invisible snow bridges and pitfalls, while Mawson followed him and the supply sledge, driven by Dr. Xavier Mertz, would brought up the rear.

On December 14, Mertz detected open space just below the surface of the snow. It was a crevasse capped by a fragile snow bridge. Before Mertz could warn the others, Mawson crossed it, but Ninnis' heavier sledge broke through the snow and plummeted out of sight. With only one sledge, six dogs and scarcely any food, the two men turned back towards their expedition's base camp over 300 miles away.

One by one they killed the dogs for food. Then, on January 8, 1913, Dr. Mertz died in their tent as they rode out a blizzard. Three days later Mawson started out for the base camp pulling the sledge behind him. For the rest of the month, he struggled on. Twice he plunged through snow bridges and found himself hanging from his sledge over a dark abyss. Painfully, he would struggle back to the surface. He would trudge on, pitch his tiny tent amidst howling blizzards and be buried beneath the snow by morning. He would then dig himself out, pack up his kit and resume his march.

With his food and strength almost spent, on January 29 he stumbled onto a food cache left by a search party. He ate, restocked and continued on, finally reaching the base on February 8. **Fight on!**

"As she was slowly forging by us not a quarter of a mile away our hearts were gladdened by the sight of the American flag, and below it an answering pennant."

A rescued seaman from the Wasash

They Saw the Flag

IN the late Nineteenth Century the British clipper, *Wasach*, was sailing to New York from the Philippines with a cargo of sugar when it was struck by a waterspout in the Celebes Sea. In a few violent seconds, the fore and mizzen masts were snapped off at the deck and carried away. The main mast was ripped wholly out of the bowels of the ship, leaving a jagged hole in the deck. Then a deluge, like a waterfall, smashed straight down on the crippled vessel. Then it was gone. Most of the provisions were destroyed. Of the 25 man crew, 14 men, including the captain and first mate, had simply disappeared. Eight feet of water filled the hold, and more poured in with each wave. Amidships the deck was almost level with the surface of the sea. The seams were opened and the remaining 11 men manned the damaged hand pumps but barely affected the water level in the hold.

The crew jury-rigged a mast and attempted to sail the 200 miles to the Sooloo Islands. But it was not to be. On the eighth day after the waterspout, a violent gale caught the ship in its grasp and sought to end its existence. The ninth morning came as their dying ship creaked and moaned its last. As the wind battered them, and the angry waves broke over them, they spied sails! A ship was going to pass near them. Their wounded vessel was so low in the water it would be nearly impossible to see in the deep troughs between the waves. Quickly they fastened their ensign, union down, to their feeble mast.

Then they sighted the American flag and a pennant answering their ensign. But they knew no boat could be lowered to their aid in such towering seas. Yet the men on the sinking hulk saw the vessel do just that. In their horror they realized their distress signal would not secure their rescue but only add these brave seamen to the death toll. But, as James J. Waite, the senior survivor put it:

> "Then we began to feel that we had done wrong in flying our signal of distress, for no boat, we thought, could live a moment in such an awful sea, and any attempt to take us off would only result in the drowning of the brave fellows who were coming to our relief, without bettering our condition a whit. They soon showed us that we were discounting Yankee skill and bravery at sea. We almost held our breath as we saw their whaleboat half lowered, the crew in place with oars apeak, and then was it dropped on the crest of a huge rolling sea when the ship lurched heavily leeward. The boat's crew slewed her quickly round head to wind as she was swept away from the ship, and let her drive down toward us with the gale, keeping her 'bows on' with the oars, and checking her sternway to meet each combing breaker. They caught the line we hove them and rode astern clear of the wash of the wallowing wreck."

The men were masterfully loaded aboard and the brave American sailors rowed them to their ship, the *Iceberg*, where with much difficulty they were put aboard and the boat secured. Just seconds later they watched the sea swallow their ship. But for bravery and seamanship, the sea would have claimed eleven more lives. **Fight on!**

Nothing Could Stop Him

ON the evening of September 16, 1868, a band of fifty tough Indian fighters led by thirty-one year old Major Sandy Forsyth camped on the banks of the dry Arikaree River. They knew there was a large band of Indians nearby and were prepared to meet them in battle the next day.

The Indians, numbering between six and seven hundred, hit the troopers at first light on the 17th. But Major Forsyth was not caught napping. He had scouted a nearby brush-covered island in the dry riverbed as a possible defensive position. As soon as the Indians hit, Forsyth double-timed his men to the island. Hordes of hostiles on horseback drove for the island, but hard men with .52 caliber Spencer repeaters blew the center out of the attack. Again and again the Indians attacked, only to be met by a wall of lead. But Indian bullets and arrows began to take their toll. Six scouts died, including the force's doctor and Lt. Frederick Beecher for whom the small island in northeastern Colorado would be named.

Major Forsyth strode around the small island instructing and encouraging his men. Suddenly an Indian bullet tore into his right thigh. Then another shattered his left leg. Yet another slammed him in the head, fracturing his skull. But nothing could stop this young, gritty commander. For the next six days he directed his men as they beat back attack after attack. It is estimated that over seventy Indians died in the encounter.

On the morning of the 25th, a relief column, led by two men Forsyth had dispatched to Ft. Wallace in Kansas, arrived to find the indomitable young commander reading *Oliver Twist* even as maggots feasted on his wounds.

When doctors wanted to amputate his legs, Forsyth fought to keep them and won. In later years he used those legs to chase Geronimo and renegade Apaches. It was as though nothing could stop him. **Fight on!**

Nothing Could Stop Them

ON the first night of what would become a nine day siege at Beecher's Island in northeast Colorado, Major Forsyth, the commander of the fifty man detachment, knew his men would not survive without relief. His horses were dead, four of his men were dead, several were wounded, and Forsyth had been shot in both legs and the head. But he still had ammunition, a good defensive position and men with a keen desire to fight.

The major needed two volunteers to steal their way on foot through the hundreds of Indians surrounding them and travel the 125 miles to Ft. Wallace in western Kansas. Nineteen year old Jack Stillwell and Pierre Trudeau, an older man, stepped forward. That night, the two slipped off their boots and stole into the blackness. Dawn found them right in the middle of the Indian encampment. They spent the day without moving a muscle and continued on when night fell. For the next two nights they avoided groups of passing Indians. On the third day they slithered into a buffalo wallow. As they lay beneath the burning sun, a large war party approached. The band dismounted just yards from them. While they held their breath, a rattlesnake decided to share their refuge with them. Unable to move against their unwelcome tenant, Stillwell used the only weapon available. He spit tobacco juice on the critter until it slithered away. The Indians soon left and so did Stillwell and Trudeau. Finally, after five days, they arrived at Fort Wallace. The men led a relief party back to Forsyth's tough band of men. **Fight on!**

Fall, Fall, Crawl

IT was June 8, 1985, and Joe Simpson and his climbing partner were rapidly descending Siula Grande in Peru after reaching its 21,000 foot summit, only to see an impending blizzard headed their way. They had descended 3,000 feet when Simpson's axe popped out of the ice and he fell 15 feet, breaking his right leg. Both men knew a broken leg on a mountain top was a death sentence. But Simpson's partner was determined to try to save him. For the next nine exhausting hours he slowly lowered Simpson down the mountain side. Suddenly Simpson began to slide and pitch off a cliff. Seeing what was happening, his partner braced himself and arrested his fall, leaving one man hanging 50 feet over a crevasse and the other trying desperately to keep both of them from being swept off the mountain. Both men called to each other, but neither could hear the other above the shrieking wind. After fighting for an hour to pull Simpson up, but unable to move him and losing his own strength, Simpson's climbing partner made a desperate decision and pulled out his knife and cut the rope. Simpson fell, landing miraculously on a small snow bridge without sustaining any new injuries. Meanwhile his guilt-ridden partner resumed his battle to descend to their base camp, battle he was certain he would lose.

Simpson took stock of his situation. He couldn't go up so he went down. He couldn't walk, so he crawled. He descended 80 feet into the crevasse below and thought he saw a glimmer of light. After two hours of agony-filled crawling, he emerged into daylight. He dragged himself two miles farther down the glacier. Now only six miles of rocky terrain separated him from camp. Crawling in 20 minute segments, he crawled for four days and finally reached the camp. He was greeted by fellow climbers, including his partner who had cut the rope and managed to stumble back into camp. It took an additional two days to get Simpson off the mountain and into a hospital in Lima, 250 miles away. **Fight on!**

"Without him, we would have lost two crucial battles, perhaps the war, and with it our freedom. He was truly a one-man army."

Gen. George Washington concerning Peter Francisco

Homeless, Not Helpless

PETER Francisco was dropped off by a ship on the dock near what is now Hopewell, VA, in June of 1765, when he was only five years old. Taken in by Patrick Henry's uncle, Judge Anthony Winston, the boy grew up in colonial Virginia. Early on it became obvious that this was no ordinary young boy. By age fifteen he was 6 foot 6 and weighed 260 pounds.

When the War of Independence broke out, Peter joined the 10th Virginia Regiment. At the Battle of Brandywine Creek he was wounded in the leg but soon recovered. He spent the winter in Valley Forge with the rest of George Washington's battered army and was then wounded again in the Battle of Monmouth Courthouse, again recovering but with a permanently damaged right thigh. Later he took a bayonet slash to the abdomen while helping conquer the British fort on Stony Point.

At the panicked colonial retreat from Camden, NJ, Francisco killed a dragoon trying to capture him and then took his horse and rode off. He came upon his commanding officer who had been taken prisoner. He killed the British guard and then gave the horse to the American colonel and told him to ride off. By this time the Redcoats had passed beyond him, and he was now behind enemy lines. Another mounted Redcoat rode up. Francisco killed him, mounted his horse, then, impersonating a Tory yelled, "Huzzah, my brave boys! We've conquered the rebels;" he charged off, back to American lines.

With his third enlistment now finished, he returned

home to Virginia, where he promptly re-enlisted in Col. William Washington's light dragoons. On March 15, 1781, Francisco killed 11 Redcoats during the Battle of Guilford Courthouse, North Carolina. He received a bayonet wound to his leg and another more grievous wound to the same leg.

Months later, functioning now as a scout, he was surrounded by nine of Lt. Col. Banastre Tarleton's calvary men. He killed two, drove off the others and rode off with their horses.

When the war ended, Francisco returned home and fought another battle - illiteracy. He enrolled himself in school at age 18 and learned to read. He died January 16, 1831, at the age of 70. **Fight on!**

The First "Top Gun"

ON Feb. 20, 1942, nine Japanese "Betty" bombers were closing in on the *USS Lexington*. Lt. Edward "Butch" O'Hare and his wingman were the only naval airmen close enough to intercept the enemy planes. O'Hare's wingman's guns jammed, so O'Hare attacked the enemy alone. In four minutes he shot down five planes and damaged a sixth. The rest fled. He had just become the Navy's first ace of World War II. O'Hare International Airport in Chicago is named in his honor. **Fight on!**

One Chance!

ON July 9, 1960, New Jersey truck driver, John Hayes, was standing at the edge of Niagara Falls, watching the water plummet over the edge. One mile up river, a drama was taking place. In a small aluminum boat were three people, 44 year old James Honeycutt, 17 year old Diane Woodward and her 7 year old brother, Roger. Honeycutt had helped build a hydro-electric plant above the falls and was showing what he had done to his two friends. While conducting his tour, their boat hit a submerged rock and sheared the pin holding the propeller. Honeycutt was no longer in control of the boat, and they were quickly swept downstream towards the falls. In the rapids above the falls, the small boat spilled its occupants into the swift moving river. Honeycutt was swept over the falls and died. Roger went over the falls and miraculously lived! He was pulled aboard *The Maid of the Mist*, the boat that supplies rides for tourists below the falls. Diane was rapidly being drawn over the falls. The young girl's cries were heard by the horrified tourists lining the railing. John Hayes saw that the girl was going to be swept over the falls at its very northern edge just below him. He watched as the girl came swiftly towards him. When he thought he had timed it right the big black man lunged out over the railing, bent down as far as he could and swept his hand down towards the fleeting young girl. At the edge of the falls their fingers touched...and locked! Hayes held on as another onlooker leaned over and grabbed Diane's other hand and the two men pulled her to safety. **Fight on!**

...And Then Some

BEGUN in 1869, the Brooklyn Bridge was the dream of German immigrant, John Roebling. Roebling died as construction was beginning and the project was taken over by his son, Washington.

To lay the foundations of the bridge, huge caissons were sunk to the bottom of the East River and pumped dry. Within these manmade caverns, workmen dug the foundation for the bridge's two great towers. Working at such a depth, many men suffered from the bends. In spite of his own poor health, Roebling would go down to inspect the work, twice collapsing in agony. Then the weight of the unprecedented project wore on Roebling's nerves. His condition confined him to his bed for the next ten years. Due to his condition, Roebling could hardly write and barely read, yet he monitored construction from his bed using a telescope, looking through the window of the bedroom of his home a quarter mile away. Roebling dictated his instructions to his wife, Emily, who carried them out. So physically and mentally drained was Roebling that he couldn't even attend the bridge's opening celebration on May 24, 1883. A grateful President Chester Arthur led a delegation to the engineer's home to thank him personally.

But this remarkable man was not "washed up." With the bridge complete, Washington Roebling fought his way back to health and successfully ran the family business until his death in 1926. **Fight on!**

Takin' er In

ON January 7, 1945, a Lancaster bomber flown by Royal Canadian Air Force Flight Officer Marshall Smith was attacked while approaching Soissons, France. Thoroughly blasted by a German night fighter, the mortally wounded aircraft began a slow spiral for the ground and right at U.S. Army troops on the ground. Smith fought for control to allow his crew time to bail out. Just short of an Army hospital, Smith, now alone, slammed all four throttles wide open. The injured bird clawed for altitude, cleared the troops, the hospital and the town of Leon, France, and then plunged to earth in a giant fireball.

No one knows exactly how many soldiers and civilians lived because, rather than bail out and save himself, Flight Officer Marshall Smith thought of others rather than himself. **Fight on!**

"....there's nothing courageous in being shipwrecked. Either you do something to save yourself, or you die. And I wasn't ready to die."

Eddy Provost

A "Human Doing"

EDDY Provost was part of a crew of three who were sailing a 38 foot yacht from South Carolina and delivering it to Newport, Rhode Island. Three days out they were overtaken by Hurricane Bob, a violent storm where 70 foot waves made short work of the yacht. As their boat sank, the three scrambled into an eight foot inflatable life raft with a seabag full of food. But the storm battered and tumbled the small boat until their supplies were swept away. The storm soon passed, but the trio was now alone at sea.

As his two crew mates fell into despair, Provost became what he called a "human doing" rather than a "human being." The former Eagle Scout caught fish by hand. He encouraged the others to dry their clothes in the sun while swimming briefly beside the raft. He would periodically pull the parachute-like sea anchor from the water and harvest seaweed, barnacles and krill for food.

Finally, eleven days after their ordeal started, they were spotted by a Coast Guard C-130 eighty miles off Cape May, New Jersey. **Fight on!**

Determination & a Dull Knife

TWENTY-EIGHT year old Aspen, Colorado, resident Aron Ralston had been shinnying through a narrow trough in the rocks of Horseshoe Canyon in southeastern Utah when an 800 pound boulder shifted, pinning his right hand. For six days he had reviewed his options and waited for rescuers to find him. Now, he knew what he must do if he was going to survive. He took out his dull pocketknife and prepared a tourniquet. Then he twisted his arm until he snapped both bones in the forearm. He hacked a gash in his arm and cut muscle, tendon and ligaments, taking care not to prematurely severe the artery. Finally, he cut the veins and artery and applied his tourniquet. Then he walked out and found two hikers. They waved down a rescue helicopter, and the long-lost hiker was whisked to the hospital. **Fight on!**

The Old Preacher's Famous Night

REVEREND Green Clay Smith, pastor of the Baptist Church in Mount Sterling, Kentucky, was a famous man. He was loved by his congregation and had even run for president in 1876 as the Temperance candidate. But his most famous and heroic act was performed on April 14, 1865, in Washington D.C. while he was a general in the Union Army.

The Civil War was over. General Robert E. Lee had surrendered just five days earlier on April 9. The citizens of Washington, as the rest of the North, were rejoicing that peace had finally come. Even President Lincoln was going to relax from his strenuous duties and take in a play at Ford's Theater. That night President Lincoln was assassinated and Secretary Seward's throat was slit while he slept in his bed. When word of these diabolical deeds hit the streets, pandemonium broke out. Citizens cried, howled and cursed...and then thought of revenge.

Imprisoned in the old Capitol were about 400 Confederate prisoners of war. Totally unaware of the evening's events, they mourned the loss of their cause but looked forward to repatriation with their families with eager anticipation. They had no way of knowing they were the target of an angry, broken-hearted citizenry. And they had no way to defend themselves.

On hearing of the evening's tragic events, General Smith, at that time the Kentucky representative to Congress, immediately surmised what was going to happen as he saw angry mobs moving towards the old Capitol. General Smith gathered a few loyal friends and told them to stall the crowd while he went for help. As his companions addressed the impatient crowd, Smith was beating on the door of Secretary Stanton. Then under orders from Stanton, the general took command of a battalion of troops, rushed to the prison and surrounded it.

Soon the mob arrived. They jeered, threatened, milled about and then, their anger spent, finally left, kept by the quick single-handed action of a saint of God from doing something they would all have later regretted. **Fight on!**

A Withdrawal of Courage

FRED Giannaros, a thin, 23 year old, Christian youth leader, was standing in line at his bank in April of 1986 when a man walked past him and knocked on the door of the manager's office. When the manager opened the door, the man, a disgruntled Marxist, drove a 10 inch knife into his stomach. As the manager dropped to the floor, his assailant launched himself at him trying to plunge the knife into his chest. Giannoros saw the injured man taking slashes to his upraised hands, and he knew he needed to act. He rushed over and threw one arm around the attacker's neck and, with the other, tried to control his knife hand. As he struggled with the deranged man, he glanced around to see which of the numerous bank customers would be coming to help. Every one had fled. He was on his own. Just then two employees grabbed the wounded manager, pulled him into the office and slammed the door. Giannoros was now alone with the crazed killer and growing tired. The two struggled for what seemed an eternity when suddenly Giannoros heard noises behind him. The police had arrived, and they took the suspect into custody.

The bank manager survived his ordeal because a quick thinking customer made a withdrawal of courage. **Fight on!**

> Come, and let us return unto the LORD: for he hath torn, and he will heal us; he hath smitten, and he will bind us up.
>
> Hosea 6:1

> And if it seem evil unto you to serve the LORD, choose you this day whom ye will serve; whether the gods which your fathers served that were on the other side of the flood, or the gods of the Amorites, in whose land ye dwell: but as for me and my house, we will serve the LORD.
>
> Joshua 24:15

A Dove Gets "Unsoiled"

THE dance hall girls of the Old West were a hard, calculating, self-centered lot, not the kind considerate fakes that Hollywood presents. The men that used them, ever wary of the term "prostitute," referred to them as "Soiled Doves." But "Vicious Vultures" would have been more accurate.

Lottie Deno was one of these predators who plied her trade in the Texas panhandle in the late Nineteenth Century. One night she waited on a table of poker players. One of the men noticed that money had disappeared and accused another of taking it. Guns appeared as everyone in the dance hall ran outside. Lottie stood by as the two quarreling gamblers blasted away, killing each other. Then she casually said, "I'm so sleepy" and sauntered upstairs to go to bed - after she counted the more than one thousand dollars she had stolen from the table.

Later, after a handsome gambler friend was killed, Lottie pinned a note to her bedspread that read, "Sell this outfit and give the money to someone in need," and left town, never to return.

She turned up in Silver City, New Mexico, where she married a gambler. But the life they lived, full of flash and dash, could not overshadow the emptiness both of them felt. One night they went to, of all things, a revival meeting. The preacher's words were hotter than any bullets that had flown around them over the years. No desperado had ever instilled fear in them as this man did, and no gold could compare to the offer he made to the congregation that night. At the end of the sermon, crowds streamed to the "Mourners Bench" to repent of their wicked ways and trust Jesus Christ as their Saviour. Among them were a New Mexico gambler and his Texas dance-hall girl wife.

The two people that left that revival were not the same two who had arrived. Rejoicing in the truth of II Corinthians 5:17, Lottie and her husband's lives changed radically. They joined the church, and for their remaining days they "walked uprightly before all men." **There's hope!**

Come now, and let us reason together, saith the LORD:
though your sins be as scarlet, they shall be as white as
snow; though they be red like crimson,
they shall be as wool.

Isaiah 1:18

For the wages of sin is death; but the gift of God is eternal
life through Jesus Christ our Lord.

Romans. 6:23

Moreover, brethren, I declare unto you the gospel which I
preached unto you, which also ye have received,
and wherein ye stand;
By which also ye are saved, if ye keep in memory what I
preached unto you, unless ye have believed in vain.
For I delivered unto you first of all that which I also received,
how that Christ died for our sins according to the scriptures;
And that he was buried, and that he rose again the third day
according to the scriptures:

1 Corinthians 15:1-4

Neither is there salvation in any other: for there is none other
name under heaven given among men,
whereby we must be saved.

Acts 4:12

For whosoever shall call upon the name of the Lord
shall be saved.

Romans 10:13

"Time and again during the course of that day, the Eve of Christmas, there were wafted towards us from the trenches opposite the sounds of singing and merry-making, and occasionally the guttural tones of a German were to be heard shouting out lustily, 'A happy Christmas to you Englishmen!'"
A British Soldier, France 1914

"They finished their carol and we thought that we ought to retaliate in some way, so we sang 'The first Noël', and when we finished that they all began clapping; and then they struck up another favourite of theirs, 'O Tannenbaum.'"
A British Soldier, France 1914

"This experience has been the most practical demonstration I have seen of 'Peace on earth and goodwill towards men.'"
A British Soldier, France 1914

How to Stop a War

ON Christmas Eve, 1914, British troops facing their German enemies over the deadly No-man's Land of France during World War I knew something was up. All day they could hear a stirring from the enemy lines. Then, here and there small pine trees began to spring up along the German line. Was it a trick? Then they heard the most unbelievable sound imaginable...Christmas carols! Across No-man's Land, the Germans had erected crude Christmas trees and then engaged in singing carols to the Prince of Peace.

Soon, the British answered back with carols of their own and cries of "Merry Christmas" sailed from trench to trench where just the day before it had been bullets making that journey.

Then, one-by-one, and in small groups, British and German troops cautiously slipped from their trenches and met reverently out on the killing fields. Along the whole front, the war was suddenly put on hold as men greeted each other, exchanged simple gifts and even enjoyed a quick game of soccer with those who had been their enemies just hours earlier. No shots were fired. No one was killed. No hatred was displayed. It was all replaced with carols and smiles and laughter. The Child of Bethlehem had done what the League of Nations couldn't, and the United Nations never will do...**He brought peace!**

Index

A

```
.45 ........................................................ 244
130 ............................................ 66, 153, 209, 290
1776 .................................................. 111, 266
abandon ..................................... 2, 25, 38, 85, 260, 262
abandoned ............. 9, 11, 25, 36, 39, 51, 82, 103, 107, 190, 191, 222
Abraham ............................................ 28, 162, 163
ace ................................................. 5, 215, 285
AC-47 ..................................................... 117
Adak ....................................................... 37
Admiral ........................................... 25, 51, 124
Afghanistan ........................................ 41, 196, 265
afloat ........................................... 138, 145, 173, 229
Africa .................................................... 138
Ahrens ................................................... 259
AH-64 ..................................................... 58
aid ................................... 101, 134, 173, 247, 276
Air Force ........................... 6, 79, 98, 193, 212, 269, 288
airborne ......................................... 41, 145, 193
aircraft ......... 2, 5, 6, 25, 26, 33, 51, 59, 61, 63, 64, 117, 118, 121, 151,
                    172-174, 179, 204, 215, 217, 218, 246, 288
airplane ............ 2, 23, 42, 59, 62, 64, 77, 98, 117, 118, 144, 151, 180,
                                                                      204
Alamo ...................................................... 9
Alaska ........................... 36, 42, 61, 79, 144, 184, 190, 252
Alaskan .................................................... 65
Albatross ................................................... 3
Aleutian .............................................. 36, 151
Alexander .......................................... 44, 45, 129
Alvin York ............................................... 244
Amarillo .................................................. 108
ambush ............................................... 95, 186
ambushed ......................................... 31, 71, 265
America ........................ 30, 41, 71, 94, 103, 110, 201, 212
American ........... 5, 11, 40, 49, 53, 70-72, 75, 84-87, 92, 93, 102, 103,
                   114, 120, 123, 125, 130, 140, 157, 160, 161, 172,
                                             254, 264, 274-276, 283
```

ammo 96, 161
ammunition 9, 25, 31, 38, 39, 48, 49, 58, 71, 73, 96, 118, 120,
175, 179, 188, 217, 218, 222, 225, 239, 279
anchor 3, 26, 63, 101, 251, 290
Anchorage 61
Andersonville 149, 150
animal 74, 108, 166, 176, 177, 204, 240, 253
Antarctic 272
Antarctica 272
ANZAC 134, 135
Anzio 160
April 3, 4, 6-8, 18, 26, 30, 77, 84, 93, 103, 106, 107, 134, 220,
225, 233, 236, 292, 294
Arab 217
arctic 104, 105, 190, 231, 262
Argonne 52, 73
Arkansas 171, 177
Army 5, 6, 9, 19, 30-32, 44-47, 52, 58, 72, 73, 79, 81, 86, 87,
92, 102, 111, 112, 117, 125, 130, 136, 158, 160,
168, 178, 180, 182, 188, 193, 205, 210, 215, 216,
222, 234, 244, 250, 265, 266, 269, 272, 282, 283,
288, 292
Arnold 251
artery 291
artillery 73, 130, 136, 160, 175, 205, 206, 217, 218, 222, 223,
268
Atlantic 74, 90, 139, 198, 220, 230, 262, 263
attack 17, 24-26, 30, 31, 38, 47, 48, 58, 71, 73, 81, 82, 85, 86,
95, 97, 109, 111, 114, 117, 119, 121, 123-125, 131,
146, 160, 166, 168, 184, 186, 209, 210, 217, 218,
222, 223, 229, 232, 240, 250, 253, 259, 277
attacked 9, 41, 44, 58, 82, 84, 95, 106, 120, 128, 130, 151, 157,
160, 184, 209, 216, 217, 228, 239, 250, 252, 253,
260, 277, 285, 288
attacking 39, 70, 102, 109, 178, 217
August 21, 111, 162, 180, 205, 209, 212, 228, 232, 250, 259,
266
Auschwitz 88, 234
Australia 135, 183, 225, 240, 250
Austria 53, 205
Austrian 205
Autrey 235
avalanche 56
avoid 12, 41
ax 79, 85
A-1 178

A-Team 9

B

Babb 176, 177
bail 77, 288
bailed 2, 46
Baptist 146, 204, 292
BAR 160, 161
Barkley 222, 223
barrel 1, 4, 17, 52, 139, 192
Bartley 144, 145
battalion 48, 73, 97, 160, 175, 293
battleship 16, 122, 123
battleships 123
bayonet 53, 97, 157, 244, 254, 259, 283, 284
bayonets 73, 97, 157
Beamer 23
bear 11, 65, 106, 109, 125, 166, 167, 184, 185, 209, 252, 253
Bedouins 120
Beecher 277
Bell 129, 145
Ben Hardy 250
Berber 97
besieged 130
Bible 82, 146, 212
Bickerdyke 108
Bladensburg 125
Blaskis 246, 247
bleeding 11, 86, 101, 168, 206, 267
blizzard 43, 46, 76, 165, 197, 253, 272, 280
blood 8, 17, 44, 49, 73, 84, 101, 118, 167, 206, 212, 225, 239, 259
bloody 10, 55, 72, 102, 103, 157
Bluffton 249
bomb 26, 77, 178, 180-182, 246, 265
bombed 217
bomber 25, 50, 178, 288
bombers 5, 59, 285
bombing 5, 6, 77, 181, 269
bombs 25, 77, 172, 174, 217, 246
Booth 68, 69
Boughton 236, 237
Boxer 53
Braddock 186
brave 23, 28, 39, 55, 150, 163, 164, 168, 183, 207, 235, 250, 254, 276, 283
bravely 10

breach 250
break 41, 106, 107, 123, 173, 234
breastworks 125
Bremerton 24
Brenn 62-64
bridge 12, 87, 93, 102, 130, 157, 158, 232, 246, 247, 272, 280,
 287
bridges 272
British 5, 11, 82, 93, 111, 112, 125, 157, 158, 186, 210, 220,
 228, 229, 254, 266, 272, 275, 283, 299, 300
Brock 170, 171
broke 12, 43, 56, 73, 79, 90, 105, 106, 131, 176, 186, 188, 195,
 197, 203, 205, 228, 240, 242, 253, 258, 263, 272,
 275, 283, 292
broken 3, 13, 30, 42, 61, 137, 143, 223, 239, 280, 292
Brooklyn 26, 111, 123, 124, 266, 287
Brown 65, 87, 109, 264
Browning 160
Buddhist 53
Buick 201
bullet 31, 106, 109, 117, 166, 169, 175, 179, 186, 225, 232, 239,
 259, 277
bullets 11, 16, 102, 121, 160, 175, 225, 226, 277, 296, 300
bunkers 48, 96
Burden 62, 114
Burgess 109
buried 17, 20, 56, 69, 134, 166, 222, 253, 272, 298
burn 12, 118
burned 1, 7, 20, 21, 26, 125, 172, 173, 195, 210, 257
burning 1, 3, 12, 25, 77, 123, 172, 174, 177, 178, 197, 245, 246,
 279
bury 199
Butler 260, 261
B-17 .... 77, 180
B-24 59
B-52 2

C

cabin 46, 76, 98, 118, 144, 165, 184, 191, 197
cabins 163
Cahill 196, 197
California 7, 248, 267
Cambodia 33
camp 9, 18, 19, 42, 81, 100, 106-109, 115, 127, 128, 143, 170,
 176-178, 184, 212-214, 233, 234, 238, 239, 250,
 252, 253, 267, 272, 280, 281
Canada 170, 232

cannon 31, 77, 186, 205, 251
Capitol 23, 292, 293
capsize 78
capsized 74, 86, 221
Captain 2-4, 7, 9, 25, 38, 47, 68, 78, 90, 91, 101, 104-106, 114,
 115, 122-124, 138-140, 149, 150, 162-164, 196,
 199, 229, 243, 251, 259, 261-263, 275
capture 29, 84, 124, 150, 160, 174, 283
captured 5, 29, 31, 33, 111, 125, 149, 177, 216, 228, 230, 244,
 250
carbon monoxide 14
Caribbean 20, 230
carjacker 249
Carlton 61-63
Carpathia 7
Carpenter 117, 118
Catalina 151
cavalry 29, 38, 39, 114, 119, 136, 205, 238
Cazneau 138-140
century 5, 79, 90, 108, 114, 128, 162, 170, 251, 275, 296
Cessna 61, 144
challenge 7, 167
challenged 73, 81
Chandler 41
Chapman 238, 239
charge 43, 72, 97, 157, 166, 168, 204, 244, 246, 261
charged 11, 38, 48, 52, 53, 71, 72, 96, 106, 119, 128, 157, 160,
 161, 204, 209, 238, 252, 253, 283
Cher Ami 175
Cherry Mine 257
Chevy 201
Chicago 113, 285
China 2, 18, 53, 141, 143
Chinese 18, 48, 49, 97, 103, 130, 131, 174
chloride... 36
Chontosh 95
Christ 156, 242, 297, 298
Christensen 109
Christian 7, 58, 62, 82, 133, 143, 244, 294
Christmas 30-32, 37, 299, 300
CH-53 33
Civil War 1, 16, 78, 136, 137, 192, 206, 216, 270, 292
Clark 3, 119
Clelland 257
Clement 173
cliff 63, 64, 84, 85, 191, 196, 197, 280
coast 25, 26, 32, 33, 66, 123, 162, 191, 198, 201, 225, 290

Coast Guard 191, 201, 290
Cocke 46
cockpit 77, 98, 179
Cody 216
coffin 127
Col. 31, 130, 131, 180, 182, 232, 233, 243, 284
cold 34, 36, 61, 97, 98, 105, 109, 120, 139, 157, 165, 168, 190,
240, 263
Colditz 214
Colonel 9, 19, 31, 130, 131, 157, 180, 181, 212, 232, 269, 283
Colorado 277, 279, 291
colors 11, 107
Colt 189
Colton 58
commander 2, 11, 31, 32, 73, 78, 84-86, 111, 117, 123, 124,
157, 210, 232, 277-279
Communist 18, 33, 48, 49, 97, 130, 201
Communists 18, 33, 103, 212
Conemaugh 202, 203
Confederate 136, 149, 150, 168, 169, 192, 206, 207, 216, 270,
292
Connecticut 189
Continental 111, 154, 266
Continentals 111
copilot 196
Corcoran 240
counterattack 17, 73, 252, 259
courage 4, 10, 12, 81, 87, 102, 111, 150, 260, 261, 294
courageous 11, 29, 260, 289
Cowra 250
craft 33, 43, 72, 77, 84, 98, 121, 151, 162, 173, 174, 179, 197-
199, 233
crash 18, 23, 178, 207
crawl 39, 66, 105, 118, 267, 280
crawled 9, 39, 52, 53, 56, 67, 102, 108, 127, 130, 161, 195, 222,
244, 267, 280, 281
Creator 153
crevasse 272, 280
crew 2, 9, 17, 21, 24, 25, 33, 36, 74, 77, 78, 90, 91, 117, 118,
139, 161, 163, 164, 181, 197, 198, 202, 220, 228,
229, 261, 265, 275, 276, 288, 290
Crocker 206, 207
cross 18, 102, 121, 212, 232, 266
cruel 129, 254, 256
cruiser 8, 123, 220
cruisers 123

Cuba 16, 102, 114, 122, 123, 201, 216
CWO 58

D

D.C. 23, 114, 210, 292
Dale 225, 226
Daly 53
damage 21, 24, 25, 78, 118, 202, 246
damaged 2, 3, 65, 102, 130, 144, 145, 197, 204, 220, 228, 246,
275, 283, 285
damaging 240, 242
David 5, 38, 98, 99, 127, 146, 173, 242, 260
Davis 1, 10
day 2, 4, 10, 12, 14, 18, 26, 34, 37, 39, 42, 43, 46, 51, 53, 55, 56,
61, 62, 74, 76, 79, 80, 87, 90, 93, 96, 101, 107, 109,
112, 115, 116, 127, 128, 134, 138, 139, 141, 150,
153, 158, 166, 172, 177, 181, 183, 191, 195, 196,
202, 203, 212, 215, 217, 218, 222, 224, 225, 230,
238-240, 248, 256, 262, 267, 270, 275, 277, 279,
295, 298-300
days 15, 16, 21, 26, 34, 43, 56, 61, 62, 72-74, 85, 86, 90, 98, 99,
106, 134, 138-140, 148, 165, 176, 193, 207, 217,
218, 240, 243, 253, 255, 257, 258, 263, 270, 272,
277, 279, 281, 290-292, 297
dead 3, 17, 25, 36, 48, 79, 89, 94, 95, 98, 139, 165, 166, 168,
170, 171, 176, 186, 206, 213, 222, 226, 227, 238,
252, 257, 259, 279
death 8, 13, 20, 47, 48, 52, 59, 71, 79, 85, 86, 97, 123, 134, 153,
160, 170, 172, 202, 203, 216, 225, 227, 232, 234,
250, 252, 254, 256, 258, 261, 276, 280, 287, 298
debris 4, 8, 172, 178, 179, 202
December 7, 24, 29, 36, 41, 56, 85, 86, 125, 131, 138, 151, 168,
182, 183, 272
deck 2, 3, 24-26, 91, 118, 172, 174, 246, 275
decks 3, 7, 24, 26, 51, 90, 172, 246
deep 14, 15, 24, 62, 63, 66, 74, 79, 99, 163, 176, 184, 198, 199,
230, 237, 238, 268, 275
deeper 14, 39, 85, 257
destroyers 51, 123, 124, 174, 247
detonated 265
Diaz 29, 201
die 5, 12, 16, 21, 35, 37, 42, 45, 54, 56, 61, 72, 74, 84, 138, 149,
154, 187, 190, 191, 227, 256, 258, 267, 289
died 3, 4, 14, 18, 20, 32, 75, 88, 91, 117, 118, 133, 134, 138,
139, 143, 153, 182, 192, 216, 218, 221, 225, 231,
232, 234, 239, 243, 247, 250, 257, 263, 267, 272,
277, 284, 287, 298

ditch 120, 178
diver 66, 67, 236, 237
divers 66, 237
division 72, 97, 182, 188
doctor 76, 127, 129, 150, 180, 227, 277
dog 79, 146, 272
dogs 71, 120, 272
Donlon 9
donut 248
Doolittle 6
door 55, 87, 105, 117, 118, 121, 163, 171, 199, 225, 249, 265, 293, 294
Doris 34, 35
drag 63
dragged 14, 21, 57, 118, 163, 242, 281
dragging 57, 183, 239
Dragoons 284
drifted 74, 84, 90, 138, 139, 199
drifting 74, 139
Duquesne 186
Dutch 90, 92, 93
dying 2, 11, 74, 76, 98, 154, 186, 216, 229, 247, 259, 267, 275

E

earthquake 7
Easley 56
Edison 255
Edward Michael 77
Egyptian 217, 218
eject 2
ejected 2
ejection 2
Emperor 216
enemy 5, 9, 11, 19, 26, 47-49, 69, 70, 72, 95, 96, 102, 117, 120, 123, 125, 130, 131, 151, 160, 174, 178, 186, 216, 222, 223, 244, 283, 285, 300
engine 25, 30, 62, 64, 101, 103, 151, 173, 185, 190, 196, 197, 202, 203
England 6, 53, 66, 92, 111, 143, 189, 231, 269
English 77, 92, 93, 140, 228, 229
Englishmen 299
ensign 16, 275
erupted 36
escape 5, 18, 26, 56, 72, 78, 87, 91, 103, 111-113, 128, 134, 171, 172, 214, 228, 229, 233, 246, 250, 257, 268
escaped 12, 33, 78, 87, 112, 131, 144, 157, 177, 233, 234, 266
Europe 180, 215, 216

Evans 16
exploded 3, 4, 8, 17, 20, 24-26, 45, 58, 77, 163, 166, 172, 178,
                                                189, 202, 227, 246
exploding 3, 25, 160, 174, 265
explosion 1, 3, 4, 24, 25, 41, 72, 98, 117, 118, 173, 174, 222
explosions 21, 172, 245

F

Fairbanks 79, 167, 184, 253
fall 11, 13, 20, 25, 44, 72, 142, 178, 218, 223, 280
fallen 11, 128, 152, 161, 169, 191
family 8, 18, 34, 103, 136, 140, 150, 171, 176, 181, 201, 267,
                                                287
farmer 240
Fasth 246
FDR 5
fear 75, 166, 177, 224, 236, 296
February 12, 24, 46, 96, 117, 120, 143, 160, 165, 201, 234, 273
fell 13, 14, 20, 21, 44, 45, 59, 77, 80, 102, 114, 119, 125, 131,
                    146, 163, 176, 191, 205, 225, 228, 235, 238, 257,
                                260, 261, 267, 279, 280, 290
fighter 79, 151, 172, 178, 215, 288
fighters 77, 151, 277
Filipino 71, 84, 85, 102
fire 1, 3, 9, 11, 12, 14, 15, 18, 21, 24, 25, 30, 33, 36-38, 46, 48,
                    49, 52, 53, 65, 68, 73, 77, 79, 84, 96, 98, 102, 106,
                    108, 120, 121, 123, 124, 130, 134, 139, 143, 160,
                    166, 172, 173, 175, 177, 178, 187, 188, 197, 205,
                    209, 218, 222, 223, 226, 228, 232, 238, 244-247,
                                250, 257, 258, 260, 270
fireman 12, 260
firemen 3, 12, 26, 36, 260
first aid 247
fish 75, 139, 263, 290
Fisher 16, 178, 179
fisherman 101
fishing 101, 190, 191
five 4, 6, 9, 15, 18, 25, 26, 48, 61, 68, 73-75, 78, 102, 104-107,
                    109, 114, 117, 118, 125, 135, 139, 145, 165, 174,
                    178, 180, 181, 183, 184, 212, 229, 230, 232, 234,
                    238, 242, 248, 254, 258, 262, 267, 272, 279, 283,
                                285, 292
flames 12, 25, 26, 36, 172, 178, 246, 257
flank 73
flanked 31
flanks 131
flare 117, 118

fleet 16, 24, 51, 112, 122-124, 174, 228, 229
flew 5, 6, 46, 61, 77, 98, 120, 130, 146, 175, 180, 196, 215, 240, 269
flight 2, 23-25, 33, 51, 77, 103, 118, 172, 173, 180-182, 196, 197, 215, 246, 269, 288
flipped 145, 212
float 117, 144
floating 25, 140
floe 105-107
flood 203, 295
Florida 201, 251
Flory 14
fly 62, 153, 166, 182, 185, 197, 210, 214, 215
flying 5, 43, 46, 58, 75, 98, 117, 121, 151, 163, 185, 196, 197, 210, 215, 276
Ford 103
Forrestal 172, 174, 245-247
Forsyth 277-279
Fort 11, 16, 38, 39, 68, 69, 184, 186, 210, 251, 267, 279, 283
Fortenberry 58
Foss 74, 75
foxhole 259
foxholes 97, 130, 134
France 53, 232, 288, 299, 300
Francis Scott Key 210, 211
Francisco 7, 98, 248, 282-284
Franklin 5, 24-27
freedom 41, 100, 150, 158, 177, 201, 231, 282
freeze 79
freezing 57, 61, 97, 98, 127
French 11, 73, 97, 158, 186, 222, 262
friend 63, 87, 109, 144, 176, 178, 183, 190, 210, 229, 248, 252, 296
friends 41, 56, 62, 89, 129, 201, 253, 286, 293
frigid 56, 79, 97, 190, 191, 240
froze 166
frozen 43, 63, 79, 104, 107, 131, 165, 191
Frye 248
fuel 25, 51, 105, 117, 172, 178, 179, 184, 185, 196, 197, 245, 246
Funchilin Pass 130, 131
fur 253
fuselage 61, 118

G

Gabreski	215
gale	36, 75, 106, 138, 275, 276
Gallipoli	134, 135
gallop	176, 248
galloped	38, 248
galloping	68, 248
Galveston	153
Gates	5
Gaza	217
General	31, 32, 38, 79, 82, 85, 103, 111, 112, 125, 130, 136, 137, 157, 158, 168, 180, 186, 206, 207, 244, 266, 292, 293
Georgia	11
German	52, 73, 77, 94, 160, 161, 175, 188, 214, 215, 220, 222, 223, 232, 234, 244, 287, 288, 299, 300
Giannaros	294
giant	202, 246, 288
Gilmore	84-86
Glick	23
God	7, 22, 29, 35, 60, 83, 89, 110, 122, 132, 152, 154-156, 163, 186, 190, 224, 225, 242, 256, 257, 261, 293, 298
Gospel	242, 298
Graham	25, 129
Grandcamp	3, 227
Grant	136, 137
Greenland	105
grenade	9, 17, 48, 49, 72, 232, 265
grenades	33, 48, 49, 52, 72, 73, 95, 130, 160, 223
Grenville	228, 229
grizzly	166, 184, 209, 252, 253
Guadalcanal	17, 254
Guam	102
guerillas	9
Gulf War	95
gun	1, 17, 25, 33, 48, 49, 52, 69, 72, 95, 117, 131, 134, 139, 160, 161, 167, 174, 205, 222, 226, 228, 232, 244, 250, 251, 285
gunboat	1
Guyton	3

H

hail	121, 187, 225
Hallowell	68, 69
harbor	3, 16, 24, 26, 31, 123, 138, 149, 162, 269
Hardey	114, 115
harpoon	75

Harris 260, 261
Hau Thai-Tang 103
Havana 123, 201
Hayes 286
headquarters 49, 244, 259
Heaven 11, 35, 187, 298
helicopter 33, 43, 58, 63, 121, 144, 145, 173, 184, 185, 191,
                                       193, 196, 197, 245, 265, 291
helicopters 12, 19, 33, 42, 58, 193, 197, 245
Hellcats 26
hero 7, 114, 134, 169, 222, 226
heroic 10, 42, 43, 118, 188, 200, 260, 292
Hess 202, 203
High Flyer 3, 4
Hoffman 46
hog 270
Holland 92, 209
Hollywood 296
Holt 216
Honduras 30-32, 201
Honeycutt 286
honor 1, 5, 9, 47, 53, 96, 116, 118, 131, 135, 136, 155, 161, 179,
                                              212, 239, 285
Hoover 5
hopeless 12, 86, 88, 100, 108, 165, 175, 199
hopelessly 91, 95, 228
horse 38, 39, 108, 119, 128, 157, 176, 184, 186, 213, 248, 283
Horseshoe Canyon 291
hospital 8, 17, 65, 101, 150, 167, 185, 191, 209, 220, 227, 234,
                                235, 237, 240, 253, 254, 281, 288, 291
hostiles 68, 277
hour 62, 63, 77, 107, 125, 153, 154, 184, 198, 216, 257, 280
hours 2, 3, 7, 9, 17, 25, 36, 39, 43, 57, 58, 62, 74, 76, 101, 120,
                         144, 146, 147, 161, 190, 191, 194, 195, 199, 212,
                                  227, 233, 234, 262, 266, 280, 281, 300
house 8, 14, 20, 54, 69, 89, 125, 163, 176, 266, 295
Howe 111, 138, 266
Huey 193
Humble 4
HUMVEE 95, 265

I

ice 7, 46, 79, 104-107, 280
Idaho 14
idea 19, 144, 189, 199, 216, 255-257
impossible 38, 75, 109, 178, 197, 275
incendiary 77, 217

independence 111, 154, 157, 159, 283
India 87
Indian 38, 44, 69, 119, 128, 177, 186, 213, 238, 239, 267, 277, 279
Indians 38, 39, 44, 68, 69, 119, 128, 176, 186, 213, 238, 239, 267, 277, 279
infantry 73, 160, 205, 215, 217, 218, 223
infantryman 160
Ingalls 5
injured 42, 56, 145, 146, 173, 178, 184, 227, 235, 245, 246, 249, 252, 288, 294
injuring 8, 18
injury 41, 76, 173
Insurrection 84, 102
invasion 29, 180-182, 205
Iowa 16, 123
Iraqi 95, 120, 121
Iroquois 7
island 20, 31, 33, 36, 71, 72, 74, 75, 96, 109, 111, 146, 151, 153, 162-164, 172, 190, 228, 251, 254, 259, 266, 277, 279, 290
islands 36, 151, 230, 275
Israel 80, 81, 217-219, 266
Israeli 217, 218
Italy 53
Iwo Jima 96, 182

J

Jackson 89, 125
Jacobs 165
January 2, 24, 47, 76, 125, 143, 157, 160, 235, 251, 271-273, 284, 288
Japan 6, 24, 53, 133, 180-182
Japanese 17, 24-26, 36, 51, 72, 96, 143, 151, 180, 182, 250, 254, 259, 285
Jasper 11
Jefferson 251
Jehu 68
Jerusalem 82
Jessop 220, 221
Jesus 153, 156, 159, 297, 298
jet 87, 98, 103, 145, 172, 245, 246
Jet Ranger 145
jettisoned 178
Jewish 88, 100, 217, 218
Jews 81, 88, 234
Johnstown 202, 203

Jonathan 80-82
journey 26, 37, 39, 85, 93, 162, 300
Joyce 114, 115
July 9, 16, 53, 59, 122, 123, 140, 172, 174, 186, 201, 245, 263, 286
jump 3, 41, 44, 64, 77, 245
jumped 19, 46, 48, 49, 95, 172, 173, 179, 185, 190, 193, 240, 249
June 38, 113, 127, 140, 198, 201, 217, 255, 280, 283
jungle 85

K

Kamikaze 24
Kansas 68, 69, 177, 277, 279
Karnes 146, 147
Kentucky 243, 292, 293
Key 210, 211, 251
Key West 251
Kidd 190, 191
kill 39, 53, 70, 85, 94, 120, 121, 130, 155, 225, 234, 257
killed 11, 17, 24, 31, 44, 47, 48, 71, 87, 102, 105, 109, 111, 125, 130, 138, 168, 172, 181, 186, 210, 213, 232, 239, 250, 263, 267, 272, 283, 284, 286, 296, 300
Kirkland 168, 169
Kirkpatrick 134, 135
Kiska 36
Knappenberger 160, 161
knife 74, 101, 128, 192, 242, 252, 253, 280, 291, 294
Kodiak 109
Korea 47, 130
Korean 18, 19, 97, 215

L

Labrador 106
ladder 44, 195, 260
Lancaster 288
ledge 63
Lee 30, 136, 144, 145, 292
legal 174
Lengel 196
Lengkeek 208, 209
Leon Compere-Leandre 20
Levi Smith 133
Liberia 204
Liddell 142, 143
lieutenant 68, 71, 79, 84, 98, 119, 123, 124, 130, 131, 169, 206, 207, 230, 232
lifeboat 220, 221

lifeboats 220, 262
Lim 260, 261
Lima 281
Lincoln 28, 103, 136, 292
Long Island 111, 146, 266
Lord 54, 62, 63, 80, 110, 146, 152, 156, 187, 219, 224, 295, 298
lost 17, 26, 41, 46, 47, 73, 93, 105, 106, 125, 138, 140, 151,
157, 162, 165, 172, 173, 175, 181, 184, 190, 192,
196, 205, 231, 232, 236, 246, 247, 253, 254, 257,
270, 282, 291
Lost Battalion 73, 175
Lottie 296, 297
Lovett 5
low 8, 51, 73, 90, 105, 139, 145, 151, 175, 179, 195, 239, 275
Lt. 33, 36, 46, 52, 59, 68, 77, 95, 98, 99, 119, 130, 131, 151,
157, 196, 197, 206, 232, 233, 272, 277, 284, 285
Lubbock 176
Luce 76, 262, 263
Luckett 43
Lucky 56, 175
Luis Grass 200, 201
Luzon 84, 85
Lyons 204

M

Macedonian 44, 45
Magred 271
mail 79
Major 69, 73, 112, 118, 178, 188, 205, 210, 212, 244, 251, 254,
265, 277, 279
Major Leagues 69
man 5, 7, 8, 10-13, 17, 21-23, 26, 31, 35, 42, 44, 48, 49, 55, 59,
62, 63, 69, 70, 72, 75-82, 85, 89, 91, 100, 103, 106-
108, 111, 112, 119, 120, 128, 131, 134, 135, 138,
141, 143, 144, 147, 160, 161, 165, 166, 168-170,
180, 182-184, 186, 187, 192, 199, 202, 203, 209,
213, 215, 222, 224, 227, 228, 231, 232, 234, 235,
237, 238, 240, 242, 244, 249, 252, 254, 257, 259,
266, 268, 272, 275, 279, 280, 282, 286, 287, 292,
294, 296
Manhattan 111
Maoist 87
March 6, 24, 26, 61, 106, 188, 201, 212, 257, 265-267, 269,
273, 284
Marine Corps 41, 95
Marines 17, 33, 41, 95, 96, 130, 141, 146, 147, 259
Mariotte 252, 253

Marshall Smith 288
Martinique 20
Marxist 294
Massachusetts 75
Mawhood 157
Mawson 272
May 14, 20, 29, 30, 33, 34, 42, 80, 91, 98, 119, 134, 139, 140,
193, 199, 202, 217, 218, 287, 290
Mayaguez 33
McCarthy 38, 39
McGrath 61
McTernan 2
medal 1, 5, 9, 47, 53, 96, 116, 118, 131, 161, 179, 212, 239,
254, 265
Medal of Honor 1, 5, 9, 47, 53, 96, 116, 118, 131, 161, 179,
212, 239
MEDEVAC 184, 265
medical 73, 134, 188, 245, 265
Mediterranean 134, 220
men 3-5, 9, 10, 14-16, 24, 25, 28, 31, 38, 39, 42-49, 52, 54, 55,
62, 63, 69, 72-74, 78-81, 84-86, 90-92, 95, 101,
102, 104-107, 111, 112, 122, 125, 126, 128, 130,
134, 136, 138, 139, 145, 147, 149, 155, 157, 161,
163, 168, 170, 172-175, 180, 182, 184, 186, 188,
197-199, 202, 206, 217, 226, 228, 229, 232-234,
238, 239, 242, 244-247, 256-258, 260, 261, 263,
266, 270-272, 275-277, 279, 280, 284, 286, 287,
296-300
Mercer 157
mercilessly 88, 210, 212
Merritt 232, 233
Mexican 29, 201
Mexicans 29
Mexico 29, 119, 170, 201, 216, 251, 296, 297
MH-60 121
Michigan 103, 209
Michmash 80-82
millionaire 243
Milwaukee 113
mines 14
miracle 111, 112
miracles 111
miraculous 112, 217
miraculously 16, 44, 76, 186, 280, 286
Miraflores 3
missionaries 143

missionary	133, 143, 204, 242
Mississippi	125, 216
Missouri	248
Mitchell	79
Mitsher	51
Mobile	78, 270
Monroe	36
monster	190
Montana	113, 195
month	21, 23, 26, 53, 99, 162, 272
months	46, 85, 86, 104, 105, 107, 139, 150, 234, 269, 284
Moody	242
Moore	166, 167
Moro	40, 71
Moros	71
Moss	264, 265
Moultrie	11
mountain	42, 43, 56, 61, 98, 99, 127, 196, 197, 280, 281
mountains	76, 85, 98, 144, 196
movie	119, 269
Mt. Rainier	127
Murphy	21
Murray	266
muskets	157
Muslim	41, 58, 87, 260
Muslims	58
Mustang	103
Myers	178, 179
M-16	95

N

natives	85, 86, 254
Navy	5, 16, 26, 31, 92, 172, 181, 191, 193, 198, 230
Nazi	234
Nepal	87
Neptune	75
Nevada	98
New Hampshire	271
New Jersey	157, 286, 290
New Orleans	30-32, 125
New World	143
New York	146, 149, 235, 262, 266, 275
New Zealand	134
Newmann	183
Nez Perce	38
Niagara	286
Niagara Falls	286

Nicaragua 201
Nicholl 74, 75
night 2, 7, 9, 17, 18, 39, 46, 51, 53, 55, 56, 61, 62, 75, 79, 82,
84, 91, 97, 98, 105, 107, 111, 112, 117, 149, 163,
164, 170, 172, 176, 177, 190, 191, 210, 213, 229,
239, 259, 279, 288, 292, 296, 297
North 18, 32, 74, 81, 103, 105, 107, 128, 149, 174, 176, 178,
201, 202, 212, 220, 260, 266, 277, 284, 292
North Carolina 149, 284
Northwest 162, 231
November 24, 30, 41, 68, 74, 118, 141, 190, 198, 220, 257, 258,
272
No-man's Land 168, 300
NR-1 .... 198, 199
NVA 178, 179

O

Oatman 267
October 24, 73, 100, 105, 109, 206, 222, 244, 255
Ogrinc 246
Ohio 8, 47, 170, 171, 186, 192, 203
Okinawa 72
Olaudah 230, 231
Olson 62-64
Ontario 188
Oregon 123
Oriskany 173, 245
overboard 36, 101, 118, 139, 173, 220, 245
O'Hare 285

P

Pacific 24, 51, 113, 181, 182, 259
Panama Canal 26
Papua New Guinea 242
parachute 59, 77, 117, 290
paralyzed 166, 240
paratrooper 182
pass 58, 77, 80, 99, 106, 117, 130, 131, 165, 242, 246, 248, 275
passengers 13, 23, 113, 138, 153, 201, 221, 262, 263
PAVE Hawk 196, 197
Peak 42, 76
Pearl Harbor 24, 26, 269
Pelee 20
Pennsylvania 202
perimeter 96
Peru 280
Philadelphia 231
Philippine 84, 172

Philippines	40, 102, 275
Philistine	81
Philistines	80-82
phosphorus	49
Pilecki	234
pilot	2, 26, 33, 42, 46, 50, 59, 61-63, 77, 78, 121, 130, 144, 145, 163, 173, 180, 184, 185, 196, 204, 215, 253, 265, 269
Piper	42, 62, 204
pistol	52, 68, 69, 89, 95, 114, 119, 138, 139, 143, 166, 167, 171, 189, 226, 238, 239
pistols	73, 100, 107, 160
Pittsburgh	186
PJ	193
plane	2, 6, 18, 25, 26, 42, 46, 51, 61-63, 77, 98, 117, 118, 144, 145, 151, 178, 179, 204
platoon	47, 52, 96, 160, 161
poison	36
poisoning	17
police	8, 31, 34, 146, 147, 226, 236, 254, 260, 294
Polish	234
Pony Express	213, 248
Poulsen	33
POW	250
pray	64, 153, 256
prayed	25, 257
President	29-32, 94, 136, 188, 287, 292
Prince of Peace	300
Princeton	157
prison	19, 55, 149, 150, 226, 233, 234, 293
prisoner	18, 84, 149, 174, 212, 214, 232, 233, 283
prisoners	11, 18, 19, 29, 33, 55, 84, 85, 88, 210, 212, 244, 250, 292
private	29, 53, 72, 114, 115, 134, 141, 155, 160, 161, 192, 215, 222, 238, 259
Providence	156
Provost	289, 290
Prussian	216
Putnam	266

Q

Queensland	183

R

radio	42, 47, 144, 173, 184, 197
raid	6, 77, 97
raiding	38, 119
railroad	30, 32, 87, 243

Ralph Jones	250
Ralston	291
Ranger	34, 46, 145
Rangers	34, 98, 165, 189
rate	26
Rebel	30, 71, 270
rebels	30, 71, 87, 92, 93, 216, 283
reconnaissance	114, 120, 151
Reddick	127
refuse	1, 10
refused	3, 16, 47, 56, 73, 107, 115, 121, 149, 161, 174, 178, 188, 192, 231, 235, 254, 262
refusing	3, 15, 175
regiment	96, 157, 160, 192, 205, 222, 232, 283
reinforcements	111
rescue	5, 11, 12, 14, 15, 18, 19, 25, 42, 53, 61-63, 75, 76, 85, 87, 91, 105, 119, 144, 151, 165, 173, 193, 197, 199, 236, 257, 276, 291
rest	2, 9, 19, 42, 74-76, 93, 96, 119, 158, 170, 184, 219, 262, 272, 283, 285, 292
retrieve	49, 56, 62, 121, 206
Revolution	31
rifle	30, 32, 48, 53, 65, 72, 106, 109, 114, 128, 130, 160, 168, 184, 223, 225, 226, 232, 244
Ritchott	194, 195
Roberts	268
Rocky	76, 84, 281
Rodebaugh	151
Roebling	287
Roosevelt	5
rope	13, 128, 164, 280, 281
Rosser	47-49
rotor	145, 196, 197
Rowland	247
Royal	230, 288
RTO	47
Rufino	12, 13
Rumbaugh	33
Russia	53

S

safe	15, 21, 87, 153, 265, 269
safety	12-14, 21, 39, 44, 46, 48, 58, 69, 76, 91, 99, 106, 107, 112, 113, 117-119, 130, 134, 135, 162, 168, 177, 187, 195, 202, 236, 238, 260, 269, 286
sailor	1, 139, 172, 173, 251
sailors	24, 26, 51, 71, 84, 104, 141, 172, 173, 245-247, 276

SAM	2, 76, 93, 189
San Francisco	7, 98, 248
Sanders	243
sang	92, 93, 212, 257, 299
sank	33, 74, 91, 145, 166, 191, 195, 220, 290
Sao Paulo	12
Sargasso	139
Saul	80, 81
savage	95, 128, 252
savages	94
Saviour	153, 297
Schaffner	52
Schmid	17
seal	74, 75, 104-107, 236
seals	74, 75, 105, 193
search	8, 15, 34, 62, 98, 144, 170, 171, 231, 273
Seattle	127
September	23, 41, 52, 71, 146, 153, 210, 220, 234, 238, 253, 260, 277
Sequoia	21
Serbia	205
sergeant	9, 38, 39, 146, 147, 161, 168, 169, 222, 244, 254, 259
Sgt.	9, 11, 38, 39, 41, 146, 168, 169, 226, 264
Shadduck	18, 19
shark	138, 139
shell	77, 79, 117, 206, 268
shelled	175
shells	25, 51, 106, 167, 210, 222, 223
Shelton	42
Shenandoah	34
shew	80
Shields	8, 45
ship	1-3, 7, 17, 25-27, 33, 71, 75, 77, 78, 90, 91, 101, 105, 107, 123, 124, 138-140, 149, 163, 172, 173, 185, 190, 197, 210, 220, 221, 229, 230, 245-247, 251, 262, 263, 265, 275, 276, 283
shoe	9
shoes	9, 63, 84
shoot	168, 226
shore	18, 71, 75, 84, 102, 112, 163
shot	5, 11, 12, 16, 25, 30, 39, 48, 49, 68, 84, 85, 93, 108, 109, 128, 160, 166, 169, 179, 186, 188, 212, 215, 222, 225, 226, 238-240, 252, 263, 279, 285
shotgun	31, 79, 225
side-wheeler	262
Sierra Nevada	98
Silver Star	212

Simpson 99, 134, 280, 281
sink 7, 26, 33, 68, 190
sinking 33, 78, 220, 229, 262, 276
Skyraider 178
skyscraper 12
slave 230, 231
slavery 230
sledge 272
sleds 79
Smallfield 59
smoke 1, 14, 15, 25, 36, 37, 98, 108, 123, 134, 146, 160, 163, 223, 257
sniper 134, 232
snow 46, 56, 57, 61-63, 79, 97-99, 106, 127, 165, 184, 196, 197, 272, 280, 298
soldier 39, 47-49, 72, 82, 115, 135, 168, 175, 206, 242, 243, 254, 264, 265, 299
soldiers 9, 11, 17, 18, 48, 49, 52, 55, 68, 72, 85, 97, 112, 114, 130, 157, 160, 168, 186, 188, 206, 222, 244, 250, 259, 288
Solomon 259
song 92, 93, 210-212
South 2, 18, 24, 74, 81, 90, 103, 107, 117, 131, 136, 137, 146, 163, 168, 202, 217, 232, 249, 259, 260, 290
Spain 102
Spanish 16, 84, 102, 114, 115, 122-124, 216, 228, 229
Spanish-American 84, 102, 114, 123
spears 68
Special Forces 9, 120, 121, 178, 193
Spooky 117
spy 107
Ssgt. 33, 146, 147
St. Joseph 248
Star Spangled Banner 210, 212
station 134, 171, 174, 243, 246
steel 97, 157, 178, 236
Steeves 98, 99
Steigel 190
Stein 96
Stewart 269
Stillwell 279
storm 36, 37, 43, 46, 90, 98, 111, 112, 127, 138, 139, 153, 162, 163, 165, 185, 190, 250, 290
Strait 201
sub 62, 66, 127, 198, 199
submachine gun 49

submarine 36, 51, 66, 198
sub-zero 62, 127
Suribachi 96
surrounded 18, 39, 53, 73, 134, 175, 176, 246, 284, 293
surrounding 279
survive 42, 59, 62, 105, 128, 154, 190, 218, 279, 291
survived 20, 31, 69, 75, 90, 101, 115, 118, 147, 153, 164, 169, 190, 209, 220, 221, 227, 234, 254, 262, 263, 294
survivor 146, 256, 267, 276
survivors 7, 14, 15, 20, 71, 73, 113, 160, 164, 173, 174, 192, 257
swam 102
Swensen 87
swim 183
swimming 75, 190, 290
sword 10, 11, 44, 45
Sydney 250
Syria 217
S-51 66

T

Tank 130, 178, 198, 199, 222, 223, 268
Tecumseh 78
telegraph 79
temperature 20, 61, 76, 127, 173, 191
Tennessee 244
tent 45, 79, 107, 149, 272
terrorists 41, 58, 260
Texas 3, 4, 29, 108, 122, 123, 128, 170, 171, 176, 189, 201, 227, 238, 296, 297
Texas City 3, 4, 227
Thompson 128
Tibbets 180-182
Tilston 188
Titanic 7, 220
Tokyo 6
tomb 56, 57, 256
torpedo 123
torpedoes 25, 198
Tortuga 251
tourniquet 291
trail 35, 46, 118, 127, 234, 253
train 30, 113, 171, 177, 203, 235
trek 84
trench 48, 49, 72, 95, 127, 300
trenches 48, 102, 112, 299, 300
Trenton 157

trestle 30, 113
trooper 29, 38, 39, 114, 119, 121, 270
troopers 38, 40, 100, 121, 134, 160, 238, 239, 277
troops 9, 19, 30, 31, 33, 44, 53, 58, 72, 73, 85, 97, 111, 120,
121, 130, 134, 149, 157, 168, 178, 188, 210, 222,
232, 266, 288, 293, 300
Trudeau 279
Tunis 78
Turks 82, 216
Tyson 105, 106
T-33 98

U

U.S. 16, 26, 27, 29, 33, 38, 39, 41, 52, 86, 103, 130, 146, 147,
160, 172, 174, 178, 182, 191, 192, 198, 201, 212,
222, 238, 243, 260, 262, 270, 288
UN 19
uniform 234
Union 1, 55, 78, 137, 149, 153, 168, 192, 206, 251, 270, 275,
292
United States 29, 30, 53, 79, 92, 93, 102, 111, 125, 133, 158,
180, 182, 201, 243, 251, 270
Utah 291

V

valley 1, 18, 82, 199, 283
Valley City 1
Valley Forge 283
Vanebo 101
Vasquez 227
vessel 1, 36, 78, 90, 91, 149, 172, 190, 199, 275, 276
vessels 191, 228
victory 44, 81, 82, 86, 93, 95, 111, 125, 128, 136, 137, 157, 158,
217, 251
Vietnam 2, 9, 103, 172, 174, 179, 193, 212
Vietnamese 9, 103, 174, 178, 212
Vigilante 170
violence 175, 259
violent 75, 84, 145, 191, 203, 275, 290
Virginia 34, 192, 206, 230, 283, 284
Vouza 254

W

Wainwright 123, 124
Waite 256, 257, 276
Walker 29
wall 44, 45, 53, 168, 169, 240, 258, 277
warrior 44, 65, 96, 120, 130, 131, 213

warriors	40, 81, 186
Washington	23, 24, 92, 110-114, 133, 136, 156, 157, 186, 210, 266, 282, 287, 292
wave	36, 101, 107, 134, 138, 145, 163, 183, 190, 275
weak	19, 55, 86
weakened	113
weakening	195
weaker	57
weapon	189, 198, 209, 250, 251, 279
weapons	52, 69, 198, 250
weather	62, 112, 272
week	15, 26, 75
weeks	66, 74, 85, 90, 91, 138, 139, 216, 272
West	21, 62, 90, 106, 113, 128, 138, 170, 189, 202, 216, 243, 250, 251, 296
white	16, 38, 86, 125, 128, 220, 230, 246, 298
whiteout	127
Whittlesey	73
Wilkenson	14
wind	36, 61-63, 76, 91, 106, 127, 144, 153, 162, 163, 183, 240, 275, 276, 280
wing	117, 144, 172, 179
wings	6, 62
winter	36, 79, 105, 190, 283
Wirtle	213
woman	8, 39, 99, 148, 149, 177, 180, 183, 220, 226, 227, 248, 262
women	88, 105-107, 176, 182, 225, 226, 262, 263
Woodward	286
World Trade	146, 260
World War I	6, 32, 36, 73, 94, 134, 220, 268, 300
World War II	6, 9, 47, 51, 59, 88, 117, 151, 172, 178, 188, 214, 234, 254, 269, 285
wound	188, 225, 284
wounded	9, 16-18, 25, 29, 33, 47-49, 71, 77, 84, 85, 96, 102, 114, 115, 118, 119, 121, 125, 134, 135, 168, 169, 173, 206, 207, 225, 226, 229, 232, 238, 239, 247, 250, 254, 265, 275, 279, 283, 288, 294
wounds	9, 16, 17, 55, 86, 118, 167, 188, 226, 247, 253, 259, 278
wreck	140, 276
wreckage	3, 8, 113, 145, 146, 178, 261
wrecked	6, 62

X

Xenia	8

Y

Yale 5
Yankee 92, 93, 174, 276
Yankee Doodle 92, 93
Yankees 93
Yosemite 165
Yuma 267

Z

zero 42, 61, 62, 76, 97, 105, 127, 151, 165, 197

Bibliography

The sources used for this book were read over a period of years. Some have been stored, some were passed on. I have not used a story that could not be documented. I have attempted to secure the correct information for each and every source. In the case of magazines, it was impossible to align each story with the correct issue. Any sources used that are not listed is purely unintentional.

I would highly recommend any book in this bibliography for your personal reading.

Air Force Magazine, April 2005, pg. 68, Nov. 2005, Dec. 2005, p.51.

Barton, David. *The Bullet Proof George Washington*, Wallbuilders, Aledo, TX., 1990.

Beyer, W.F. and Keydel, O.F. *Acts of Bravery, Deeds of Extraordinary American Heroism*, Longmeadow, Stamford, 1993.

_____ *Big Ben the Flat Top*, Albert Love Enterprises Publishers, 1990 reprint, Atlanta.

Canning, John. *Great Disasters - Catastrophes of the Twentieth Century*, Gallery Books, New York, 1976.

Car & Driver, August 2006.

Carmony Neil O., Brown, David E. *Tough Times in Rough Places*, University of Utah Press, Salt Lake City, 2001.

Cavendish, Marshall. *Escape from the Swastika*, Golden Hands Books, London, 1975.

Clark, Johnnie M. *Gunner's Glory*, Ballantine, New York, 2004.

Collinson, Frank. *Life in the Saddle*, University of OK Press, Norman, 1963.

Convis, Charles L. *Miners*, Carson City, NV, Pioneer Press, 1998.

Cooke, Donald. *For Conspicuous Gallantry*, Hammond and Co., Maplewood, NJ, 1966.

Cumming, Joseph. *The Greatest Search and Rescue Stories Ever Told*, Lyons, Guilford, CT., 2002.

Dary, David. *True Tales of the Old Time Plains*, New York, Crown, 1979.

Dear, Ian. *Escape & Evasion*, Cassell & Co., London, 2000.

Douglas, Tom. *Great Canadian War Heroes*, Attitude Publishing, Alberta, 2005.

Duff, Xavier. *Accidental Heroes*, Five Mile Press, Victoria, Australia, 2005.

Evans, David. *Random Acts of Kindness*, Wilmington, NC, Broadfoot, 2001.

Farabee, Charles R. *Death, Daring and Disaster*, Rinehart, Lanham, MD. 2001.

Faryon, Cynthia J. *Unsung Heroes of the Royal Canadian Air Force*, Attitude Publishing, Alberta, 2003.

Feldt, Eric. *The Coast Watchers*, Angus & Robertson, Melbourne, Australia, 1946.

Freeman, Gregory A. *Sailors to the End*, Avon, NY, NY, 2002.

Garrison, Webb. *A Treasury of Texas Tales*, Rutledge Hill Press, Nashville, 1997.

Garrison, Webb. *Civil War Curiosities*, Rutledge Hills Press, Nashville, TN, 1994.

Greene, Bob. *Duty*, Perennial, NY, 2000.

Griffith, Samuel B. II. *The Battle for Guadalcanal*, Bantam Books, NY, 1980.

Guenter, Abe. *Jungle Pilot in Liberia*, Regular Baptist Press, Schaumburg, IL., 1992.

Guttman, Jon. *Defiance at Sea*, Rigel, London, 1995.

____ *Hero Tales of the American Soldier and Sailor*, Century Manufacturing Co. Philadelphia, 1899.

Hirsh, Michael. *None Braver*, New American Library, NY, 2003.

Hornfischer, James D. *The Last Stand of the Tin Can Sailors*, Bantam Books, NY, 2004.

Jacobs, Bruce. *Heroes of the Army*, NY, Berkley, 1956.

Law, Anwie Skinsnes. *The Great Flood*, Johnstown Area Heritage Assoc., Johnstown, 1997.

Lawrence, Richard Russell. *The Mammoth Book of Storms, Shipwrecks and Sea Disasters*, Carroll & Graf, NY, 2004.

Letterman, John B. *True Tales of Endurance,* Simon & Shuster, NY 2003.

Lewis, Jon E. *The Mammoth Book of True War Stories*, Carroll and Graf, NY, 1999.

Long, Ben. *Great Montana Bear Stories*, Helena, Riverbend Publishers, 2002.

MacKenzie, Catherine. *Alexander Graham Bell, The Man Who Contracted Space*, Grosset & Dunlap, NY, 1928.

Mason, Philip. *Niagra and Its Daredevils*, Niagra Daredevil Gallery, Niagra Falls, 1969.

McCullough, David. *1776*, Simon & Shuster, New York, 2005.

McKinney, Mike and Ryan, Mike. *Chariots of Death*, St. Martin's Press, New York, 2001.

Minutaglio, Bill. *City On Fire*, Harper Collins Publishers, New York, 2003.

Mueller, Larry T. Reiss, Marguerite. *Bear Attacks of the 20th Century*, Guilford, CT., Lyons Press, 2005.

National Geographic, Vol. 163. No.5, May 1983.

Neider, Charles. *Man Against Nature*, NY, Harper & Brothers, 1954.

O'Leary, Col Jeffery. *Taking the High Ground*, Victor, Colorado Springs, 2001.

Pisor, Robert. *The End of the Line*, Ballantine Books, NY, 1982.

Rosenbaum, Robert A. *Best Book of True Sea Stories*, New York, Doubleday & Co., 1966.

Searl, Molly. *Montana Disasters*, Boulder, Pruett Publishing, 2001.

Settle, Raymond W., Lund, Mary. *Saddles & Spurs*, Un. of Nevada Press, Lincoln, 1955.

Shaw, David W. *The Sea Shall Embrace Them*, NY, The Free Press, 2002.

Snow, Edward Rowe. *Great Gales and Dire Disasters*, Dodd, Mead & Co., NY, 1952.

Smith, Robert Barr. *To The Last Cartridge*, Robinson Publishing, London, 1994.

Stark, Peter. *Ring of Ice*, Lyons Press, Guilford, CT., 2000.

Swift, Catherine. *Eric Liddell*, Bethany House, Minneapolis, 1990.

_____ *The Story of the Great War*, P.F. Collier & Son, NY, 1916.

Tintori, Karen. *Trapped*, Atria Books, NY 2002.

Vyborny, Lee & Davis, Don. *Dark Waters*, New American Library, New York, 2003.

Walker, Spike. *Nights of Ice*, St. Martin's Griffin, NY, 1997.

World Magazine, April 16, 2005.

Wright, David & Zoby, David. *Fire on the Beach*, Scribner, NY, 2000.